The Greatest Navy SEAL
Stories Ever Told

THE GREATEST NAVY SEAL STORIES EVER TOLD

LAURENCE J. YADON

Guilford, Connecticut

An imprint of Globe Pequot

Distributed by NATIONAL BOOK NETWORK

British Library Cataloguing in Publication Information available

Library of Congress Cataloging-in-Publication Data
Names: Yadon, Laurence J., 1948– author.
Title: The greatest Navy SEAL stories ever told / Laurence J. Yadon.
Description: Guilford, Connecticut : Lyons Press, [2018] | Includes bibliographical references.
Identifiers: LCCN 2018003822 (print) | LCCN 2018015962 (ebook) | ISBN 9781493030903 (Electronic) | ISBN 9781493030897 (pbk. : alk. paper)
Subjects: LCSH: United States. Navy. SEALs—History. | United States. Navy. SEALs—Biography. | Special forces (Military science)—United States—History. | Special operations (Military science)—United States—History.
Classification: LCC UA34.S64 (ebook) | LCC UA34.S64 Y33 2018 (print) | DDC 359.9/84—dc23
LC record available at https://lccn.loc.gov/2018003822

♾™ The paper used in this publication meets the minimum requirements of American National Standard for Information Sciences—Permanence of Paper for Printed Library Materials, ANSI/NISO Z39.48-1992.

Dedication

To the Navy SEALs who have lost their lives, often in remote, lonely places for the America we love and in memory and honor of my coauthor, Robert Barr Smith, soldier, scholar, writer, loyal friend, and American patriot.

CONTENTS

Author's Note

SEALs in action—from the rice paddies and hills of Vietnam to the plains and mountains of Afghanistan, Iraq, and Pakistan—appear in these pages. These stories cover the most significant overt and covert operations conducted since the U.S. Navy established the SEALs on January 1, 1962. The one common denominator in these chapters is the courage and ingenuity of those who proudly call themselves Navy SEALs. Sometimes SEALs and other participants in these stories recall differing versions of the same events. Those variations are recounted here for the reader to make his or her own judgments. As far as I know, no previously classified or sensitive information is revealed in these pages.

Many of the terms and place-names described in this book have multiple spellings. Al-Qaeda for example, can be spelled in English twelve different ways. I have attempted where possible to use the most common spelling used in sources such as the *New York Times* and the *Wall Street Journal*. Also some spelling conventions, such as those used describing military operations, have changed through time. I have discarded the American typographic convention of capitalizing operation names in their entirety on the assumption that most readers prefer clarity at the expense of strict historical accuracy. The operations span Europe, Africa, and the Middle East from World War II to the current fight against ISIS.

CHAPTER ONE

Creating the SEALs

ALTHOUGH PRESIDENT JOHN F. KENNEDY IS SOMETIMES SAID TO HAVE established the U.S. Navy SEALs, in fact he did not. Shortly after taking office on January 29, 1961, the new president did urge Navy leadership to accelerate already existing plans to initiate a marine counterpart to the U.S. Army Green Berets. Soviet Premier Nikita Khrushchev vowed in early January 1961 before Kennedy was inaugurated that the Soviets would support wars of liberation and popular uprisings worldwide. During a February 23, 1961, meeting with the Joint Chiefs of Staff only weeks after he became president, Kennedy stressed the importance of developing guerrilla and counterguerrilla warfare options in response to communist tactics in Southeast Asia and elsewhere. And Kennedy, a U.S. Navy veteran of close-quarters World War II combat, wanted these new warfare options in place as soon as possible. Less than three weeks later, a recently formed Unconventional Activities Committee within the Navy proposed two such units, one for the Atlantic and one for the Pacific, to be known as SEALs, a contraction of "Sea, Land, and Air" designed to emphasize their all-around, universal capability. The term was apparently coined by Rear Admiral William Gentner or someone on his staff unidentified to this day.

In one version of events, President Kennedy asked during a January 1, 1962, National Security Council meeting whether the Navy had anything comparable to Army Green Berets. "We have our SEALs," the Navy representative told him, and by the end of that very day, SEAL Teams One and Two, already in the last stages of planning, were officially established. That may have happened, but Admiral George W. Anderson signed CNO Speedletter # 697P30 directing that very action and effective date twenty-one days earlier in early December 1961. And such new tactics had been discussed within the Navy for years. The details of the backstory are worth recounting.

American military leaders began discussing new methods of combating guerrilla warfare in the late 1950s. Finally, during the last months of the Eisenhower administration on July 11, 1960, Admiral Arleigh Burke, Chief of Naval Operations, directed that units trained in guerrilla warfare be studied and organized. William M. Burke's deputy, Admiral Beakley, responded that August, suggesting that the Navy Underwater Demolition Teams (UDTs) and Marine Reconnaissance Units be considered for conducting the new mission.

The Unconventional Activities Working Group that was tasked that September reviewed innovative methods, techniques, and concepts to be deployed against Sino-Soviet opponents. Admiral Burke advocated that the Navy prepare itself to wage as much guerrilla war as possible, led by a cadre of young naval officers to be trained by the Army at Fort Bragg.

After Kennedy became president, in March 1961 the Strategic Plans Division of the Committee on Unconventional Activities recommended that the SEALs be comprised of twenty to twenty-four officers and fifty to seventy-five men who would develop a specialized Navy capability in guerrilla and counterguerrilla operations, supporting tactics, and specialized support equipment.

After the mid-April 1961 Bay of Pigs debacle in Cuba, Defense Secretary Robert McNamara asked for new ideas on "counteraggression." President Kennedy directed a lessons-learned review and search for ways to strengthen military, paramilitary, guerrilla, and antiguerrilla capabilities just short of overt war. After several months of delay, Burke's successor, Admiral George Anderson, signed a directive activating SEAL Teams One and Two, effective January 1, 1962. Navy officers William Henry Hamilton Jr. and Roy Boehm were particularly instrumental developing the SEALs' methods and standards.

Captain William Henry Hamilton Jr., then assigned to UDT 21, wrote a letter to Admiral Burke from the UDT base at Little Creek,

Virginia, suggesting that the Navy work with the Army Special Forces developing the capabilities that President Kennedy wanted. Eventually, Hamilton began assembling the men, money, and materials needed to build the SEALs. In the Pentagon, Admiral Don Griffin helped Hamilton clear obstacles and bureaucratic hurdles within the Navy along the way. Among other tasks, then Commander Hamilton drove 324 miles to Fort Bragg to acquire unconventional and counterguerrilla manuals and training materials. Hamilton did much of the heavy lifting in the buildup of SEAL Teams One and Two, initially with personnel acquired from the Navy UDTs. Eventually, Hamilton became chief of Central Intelligence Agency (CIA) maritime operations.

Commander Roy Boehm, the operations officer for UDT 21, began organizing a SEAL commando unit in 1962. He assembled men from within that unit and then initiated training based in part on the writings of revolutionaries such as Che Guevara and Mao Tse Tung and the military strategist Sun-Tzu. He also studied the work of U.S. Admiral Milton Miles, who commanded Navy forces training Chinese guerrillas in small arms, demolition, and sabotage for World War II operations against the Japanese. Boehm had prior experience training and sending "anytime, anywhere" UDT operators in teams of two on sensitive covert missions.

After UDT 21 operators became SEAL Team Two, stationed at Little Creek, Virginia, some twenty miles west of Virginia Beach, Boehm searched for the most suitable arms and equipment, regardless of price or strict Navy purchasing rules. He quickly settled on the Armalite AR-15, predecessor of the M-16. Boehm also ordered custom-made parachutes and even some British crossbows for silencing sentinels, stirring up arguments with testy Navy purchasing officials along the way at no small risk to his military career.

These purchasing problems plagued even the most sensitive operations. Boehm later recalled that breathing equipment he carefully selected for a highly secret beach reconnaissance mission in Cuba was derailed. One of the "low bidder" standard-issue replacement rigs issued to the SEALs failed during the operation just as two Cuban boats approached them. Boehm and his men managed to finish the mission and return to their submarine just before the Cubans began another sweep of their area.

"I didn't vote for you, but I'm willing to die for you," said Boehm when he first met President Kennedy several months earlier. Despite this, Kennedy arranged for purchasing-related court-martials against Boehm to be dropped. He also arranged a promotion.

SEAL Team One became "One" simply because commanding officer David Del Guidice completed and turned in the necessary paperwork twelve minutes before Lieutenant John F. Callahan, his counterpart in what became SEAL Team Two, did. Just two months before, Callahan began picking the officers and men for his new unit. Half of the officers Callahan selected began their careers as enlisted men, called "Mustangs" then and now. Many of the rest consisted of freshly graduated officers, complimented by seasoned enlisted men from the UDTs. Some volunteered for the SEALs simply to get parachute training, having no idea what the SEALs' missions might be. The assigned training in survival, jungle warfare, signal coding, escape, and evasion answered any questions those recruits might have about future operations.

Basic Underwater Demolition/SEAL TEAM (Bud/s) Training was and is the most rigorous training of its kind in the world. The normal attrition for the twenty-week course according to one 1972 source was 66 to 75 percent. Phase I includes physical training, obstacle courses, night problems, and constant running. During Hell Week (week 5), candidates did not sleep at all.

Only those who have completed a SEALs or Demolition Training Replacement course are entitled to wear the Navy Special Warfare Breast Insignia, known as the Trident. In the early days, enlisted men wore silver, but now all wear gold. A spear representing Neptune, god of the sea, is crossed with an anchor, a pistol, and a flintlock, representing readiness, just below an emblematic American eagle. And as we shall see in the next chapter, the story of the Navy SEALs really began a year before World War I erupted.

CHAPTER TWO

Before the Seals

Scouts, Raiders, and Sailors

"What the hell am I doing here?"

FEW AGREED WITH MARINE LIEUTENANT COLONEL EARL HANCOCK "Pete" Ellis when he predicted in 1913 that someday the Japanese and the United States would battle in the Pacific. Yet when the seemingly invincible Japanese monolith began moving across the Pacific twenty-eight years later, the Navy dusted off Operational Plan 712H, which Ellis himself prepared in 1921. And that report served as the basic strategy for Marine amphibious operations throughout World War II, beginning with the first U.S. landing craft used in Operation Watchtower, the August 2, 1942, Guadalcanal operation that met little Japanese resistance.

Twelve days later, a costly Allied raid on Dieppe in northern France convinced the American military leadership that successful amphibious operations would require more men with specialized training than they had planned for. Naval Construction Battalions, later known as the Seabees, began shortly after Pearl Harbor. A Joint Amphibious Scout and Raider School, initially established at Little Creek, Virginia, in July 1942, trained soldiers and later sailors in the use of small boats and landing craft, navigation, and scouting. The Navy contingent received similar but not identical training preparing the sailors to locate, scout, and occupy targeted beaches in advance of large-scale invasions. After moving to Fort Pierce, Florida, the Scout and Raider School became an all-Navy enterprise in December 1943.

The first combined-force amphibious mission launched Operation Torch during the early November 1942 Allied invasion of North Africa. A detachment of Scouts and Raiders marked and lighted Moroccan landing beaches at Fedala. That same day, a combined force of Army and Navy Raiders launched a mission to secure a critical airfield at Port Lyautey, some seventy miles inland from the Atlantic.

The Vichy French expected them and obstructed the Sebou River with a heavy cable and, by some accounts, a net. Machine gunners waiting in ambush along the cliffs above the river drove them away once, but they tried again in the late darkness of Monday, November 9. They cut the cable by 2:30 the next morning, but intense machine gun fire forced them to retreat. Finally, on November 10, the Americans secured Port Lyautey, even as others prepared new plans for amphibious operations and tactics. The success there encouraged American Army and Navy leadership to include Naval Scout boat crews, Army Scouts, and Raiders as essential elements of the Allied invasions that followed.

This would be no easy task. Axis forces anticipated at least two invasions and prepared key beaches accordingly, even as the U.S. Navy developed obstacle clearance techniques. Newly designated and formed Naval Combat Demolition Unit # 1 began training in mid-1943 for the Husky operation, which prepared three beaches for the July 10, 1943, invasion of Sicily. In the meantime, a second unit trained at Fort Pierce for service in the southwestern Pacific.

Four months later, the November 1943 Tarawa Atoll invasion was hampered by withering fire from Japanese fortifications that should have been destroyed, by reefs not scouted, and by unanticipated shallow waters restricting the landing craft. Drowning killed more Marines than Japanese small-arms or artillery fire. Rear Admiral Richmond Kelly Turner swore that the Navy would learn from these mistakes. And it did.

The Fifth Amphibious Force began training that very month at Waimanalo, Oahu, in Hawaii, a world away from Terrible Tarawa, clearing obstinate coral formations and mines from beachheads. Two UDTs were ready for action by January 1944. UDT 1 and 2, comprised of sailors from Naval Combat Demolition Units (NCDUs) trained at Fort Pierce, went to Waimanalo one month earlier than projected. The new UDTs each included fourteen officers and seventy enlisted men. UDT 2 soon joined the invasion of Roi and Namur in the Marshall Islands.

UDT teams flawlessly performed in two separate missions on February 1, 1944. Many years later, Commander Robert P. Marshall recalled conditioning good swimmers from the previously existing NCDUs to do long offshore reconnaissance missions. By the end of the training, Marshall and the others swam to locations as far as ten miles away. They also trained to do more detailed reconnaissance to eliminate or mitigate the reefs and tidal miscalculations that caused the Tarawa debacle, with newly developed techniques using string and reels improvised from fruit cans.

June 15, 1944, found UDT 2 at Saipan, spread out over 600 yards on beach "Green" tasked to reconnoiter the offshore waters under heavy but largely ineffective enemy machine gun fire from so far away that most of it bounced off the waves. Even so, one man died.

Earlier that month, the original NCDUs graduating from Fort Pierce prepared the Normandy beaches for the June 6 invasion of France. Since a small number of NCDU teams had to clear so many obstacles, they improvised a solution. Combined Army/NCDU units consisting of Army combat engineers and mostly new seamen designated as Gap Assault Teams took on some of the most difficult missions.

Five years earlier, Belgium installed thousands of barricades along the thirty-seven-mile line between Koninghooikt and Wavre to deter a potential tank invasion. These "Belgian gates," typically ten feet wide, ten feet high, and fourteen feet long, featured concrete rollers linked together by steel cable and then configured in a zigzag pattern. French Colonel Leon-Edmond de Cointet de Fillian designed the devices in 1933 for the Maginot Line.

During the May 1940 German invasion of Belgium, the 3rd and 4th Panzer divisions quickly found gaps in the Maginot Line caused by a planning snafu. The German occupiers deployed some 23,000 of these

Belgian gates (also called Cointet barriers, C-Element, or Element C) over some 2,700 miles of coastline to repel Allied invaders.

During early Allied reconnaissance, Lieutenant Carl Hagensen, part of a Navy team assigned to overcome these obstacles, discovered that these Belgian gates could be destroyed by plastic explosive Composition C-2. They poured the compound into wool socks, bundled the socks into canvas bags, and connected the bags with detonating cord. The team assembled thousands of these "Hagensen Packs" for the Utah and Omaha Beach assaults in Normandy. Utah was as easy for the amphibious Allied operators as Omaha was difficult. The NCDUs sustained 50 percent casualties at Omaha.

Myron Walsh later recalled how his unit, NCDU 127, prepared in England for the Normandy invasion. They worked with Army engineers in a farm field near Salcombe assembling Hagensen Packs. One night, cows ate some of the sweet-tasting C-2 left on tables, but NCDU operators stuffed the rest into knapsacks and lugged them to Normandy on landing craft. During the operation, several Allied rockets collided and fell toward Walsh's landing craft, forcing the coxswain to maneuver them out of harm's way to avoid being blown up before reaching their destination, just off Omaha Beach.

"Okay, this is where you guys get out," the coxswain said minutes later, ordering Myron Walsh and three other warriors into five feet of water, lugging forty-pound Hagensen Packs. Two luckier team members jumped into a rubber boat as the tide rolled them all toward Utah Beach and German machine gun fire. Between salvos from 88-mm guns landing in the water nearby, Walsh and the others rowed the rubber boat as quickly as possible toward shore. Once there, they moved inland, jumping into holes dug by defending artillery fire along the way, cutting a fifty-yard path through some 200 yards of Belgian barricades, logs, and land mines before the main Allied force arrived. After that, they became beach traffic cops.

A far worse assignment loomed ahead. After clearing beach obstacles, Walsh and his comrades went back into the water for twenty-foot dives down double rows of posts and pilings twenty to thirty feet from shore, carrying enough explosives down in the darkness to destroy a tank.

Frank Meder joined in the last amphibious operation of World War II on July 4, 1945, in Borneo. Meder started in a Fort Pierce UDT class of about 750 reduced to eighty by graduation in October 1944. Meder and the others traveled to Maui for the swimming component of their training.

Then Meder and his team began the journey to the southwestern Pacific. There, UDT 18 operated with the Seventh Australian Division, doing daily hit-and-run operations to keep the Japanese off guard; the enemy had no choice but to reinforce troops on numerous beaches without knowing which specific beaches would be Allied assault targets. On their last mission of the war, UDT 18 prepared the beach for American troops on July 4 at 150-foot intervals. Meder recalled later bailing out of the team rubber boat after tossing floating bag charges into the water. More than once, while towing a hundred pounds of explosives to the beach under heavy fire, he asked himself, "What the hell am I doing here?"

Years after the Normandy invasion, coxswain Joe Martino of Navy UDT 25 remembered praying constantly at Omaha Beach, dodging artillery rounds as he steered a rubber boat. Martino stayed in the Navy after World War II, attended Army jump school at Fort Benning, and parachuted out of a C-119 Flying Boxcar, dubbed "the Bumblebee." He accepted a limited-duty officer commission that year, joining SEAL Team Two, comprised of ten officers and ten enlisted men, at Great Lakes Naval Training Station in Illinois in early 1962.

Martino's fifteen years scuba diving, sky jumping, and conducting helicopter operations in Underwater Demolition Units prepared him for future missions in the SEALs. The hydrographic reconnaissance and obstacle demolition that UDT members like Martino did during World War II became secondary in Vietnam. There, the primary mission of the SEALs became marine operations and going behind enemy lines to infiltrate or gather intelligence, as described in Kevin Dockery's 2002 book *Navy Seals II: The Viet Nam Years*, relied on in this chapter. The Escape and Evasion School at Bridgeport, California, taught particularly critical skills and an overriding mandate for SEALs to live by in Vietnam: don't be captured.

Marine instructors conducted the school, sometimes playing communist captors during lengthy training sessions. The trainees learned that if they were captured, the pain would never end.

SEAL Team Two deployed to the Dominican Republic Crisis during a 1965 crisis there. President Lyndon B. Johnson sent some 22,000 troops on April 28 to establish order and forestall a possible communist takeover. The Organization of American States troops equaled the American forces in numbers. Team Two went to Santa Domingo on a C-7 Caribou cargo plane too late for any heavy action, but team member Captain Thomas N. Tarbox, who didn't really want to be a SEAL, deployed separately. Tarbox spent his childhood in Montana and Colorado; too short to become a Navy pilot in that era, he elected to join the UDTs while still in Officer Candidate School. He joined Class 19 at Little Creek, Virginia, in January 1958 and witnessed two tragedies in later operations. While Team Two trained in 1963 off the coast of Turkey, a fellow officer dove into the Bosporus alone and against the rules, never to surface.

Chapter Three

The Forest of the Assassins

WHEN SEAL DEPLOYMENTS BEGAN, TEAM ONE INCLUDED SOME FIFTY men and five officers from UDT 11 and 12. SEAL Team Two, with the same compliment of enlisted men but ten officers, came mostly from UDT 21. The first SEALs arrived in Vietnam that July to perform reconnaissance missions in the Rung Sat Special Zone (RSSZ), which some South Vietnamese called the Forest of the Assassins.

During the Vietnam War (1955–1975), the Navy SEALs conducted some conventional operations but also focused on special operations, capturing or killing Vietcong (VC), and conducting American prisoner-of-war (POW) rescues. Lenny Waugh became one of the first SEALs deployed to Vietnam in early 1962 as part of a Team One detachment training nationals in underwater scouting, demolitions, and reconnaissance. Back at Coronado, he helped train Vietnamese Navy Seals. When Team One began Vietnam combat missions in 1966, Frank Toms deployed to Da Nang as part of UDT 11, which did beach surveys from early morning to late at night all along the Vietnam coasts in missions lasting as long as two weeks. From time to time the SEALS ambushed the VC at night using knives instead of rifles. On one such mission while boating to an ambush, Toms's landing craft (a Landing Craft, Personnel [Large]), was struck by a wave or a sampan. That blow jammed a Stoner machine gun into the firing position, killing Toms's friend, Navy SEAL Walter Pope, with his own weapon.

During Operation Jackstay, which began in April 1966 (the first amphibious landing during the Vietnam conflict), thirty-one-foot river patrol boats of that era sported three .50-caliber machine guns and at least one M60 for protection.

In the months that followed, SEALs conducted hit-and-run, reconnaissance, and intelligence operations against the VC in the RSSZ. In one such operation, Team One killed some eighty-six VC and destroyed some thirty bunkers, but the VC soon retaliated. That October 7, a large VC force mortared American squads in boats, causing seventeen casualties, but forty enemy forces died. Soon, the SEALs began to participate in the most controversial American operation of the Vietnam War.

The Intelligence Coordination and Exploitation Program began in 1967. Senior CIA officer and 1949 Yale graduate Nelson Brickham modeled the program on strategy and tactics that David Galula developed during the Algerian War (1954–1962) and documented in the 1964 Galula book on counterinsurgency warfare. SEAL veteran and prolific writer Dick Couch described those early missions with the South Vietnamese Provincial Reconnaissance Units (PRUs) to be among the most successful SEAL operations of the war. Later, the CIA-sponsored PRU operations were merged into an organization called Phoenix. The Phoenix leadership model loosely followed the Ford Motor Company executive structure of that time. The Phoenix goal: disrupting the VC leadership structure. In a 1967 interview, one SEAL described the primary mission as capturing and interrogating VC, killing VC only when particular operations were compromised.

The South Vietnamese PRU forces financed by the CIA and advised by Army Special Forces Marines and SEALs recruited extensively among Nung tribesmen of Chinese origin. Combat-hardened SEALs typically operated alone and "advised" sixty to 120 Nung fighters at a time, often in remote villages. SEALs also participated directly in Phoenix program operations.

No one disputes the effectiveness of Phoenix, as confirmed after the war in communist documents. Phoenix program historian and critic Dale Andrade acknowledged in his fine book *Ashes to Ashes: the Phoenix Program* that PRUs led by SEALs effectively eliminated a significant amount of VC infrastructure. Although innocent civilians died as well, Andrade considered this to be inevitable since the VC intentionally wrapped themselves in the civilian population.

Night assassinations later became synonymous with Phoenix, justifiably or otherwise. The PRU numbered fewer than 5,000 yet neutralized more VC infrastructure than all other such South Vietnamese units combined. They originated in counterterrorism teams that CIA Far Eastern Division Chief William Colby redesignated as PRU in 1966. The name change minimized the "killer image" of the teams, but nothing else changed.

Recruiters made word-of-mouth contacts with villages in which family members were killed by VC. They operated in small groups—one platoon usually comprised of three squads in each province. This maximized security and allowed the PRU to surprise the VC in operation after operation small enough to avoid major communist buildups.

The PRU effectively developed independent, largely reliable intelligence sources. Generally, they conducted small-scale operations, such as hit-and-run missions involving no more than two squads. Despite its original stated mission, more often than not the PRU killed rather than captured intended targets.

In one known December 1969 incident in Quang Tri province, they captured eight district-level VC principals and shot them all without interrogation, angering CIA and American military advisers who considered this to be a lost intelligence-gathering opportunity. That said, the Americans leveraged PRU brutality, persuading captured VC shadow government officials and soldiers to become informers.

In January 1967, SEAL Team One sent specially trained Detachment Bravo to assist the PRUs on highly classified "infrastructure" missions. These SEALs did not merely advise. Instead, they actively led "snatch" missions, conducted mostly at night, deep in VC territory, turning the tables on communist insurgents who never knew where or when the SEALs would strike.

Two years later, Lieutenant Joseph "Bob" Kerrey led Delta Platoon, SEAL Team One, based near Nah Trang Harbor on the South China

Sea, in a mission targeting VC leadership but not associated with Phoenix. Kerrey, a native of Lincoln, Nebraska, joined the Navy despite a lifelong asthmatic condition that might have exempted him from military service. He began as a seaman, went through Officer Candidate School, and applied for underwater demolition training at Coronado at age twenty-four. Two of his classmates drowned during the course, but Kerrey and eleven others received invitations to join SEAL Team One. During the January 1968 Tet Offensive in Vietnam, Kerrey prepared for Rangers and Airborne schools at Fort Benning, Georgia. January 1969 found Kerrey flying across the Pacific to Cam Ranh Bay, on the South China Sea, headquarters for American coastal patrols using new vessels called swift boats. Typically fifty-footers powered by diesel engines and equipped with machine guns and mortars, these boats originally served oil rigs in the Gulf of Mexico.

The SEALs whom Kerrey's platoon replaced had operated in the Mekong Delta, so Kerrey began operations along Cam Ranh Bay without any actionable intelligence. Their mission: abduct VC soldiers for interrogation and conduct ambushes. Kerrey and the other SEALs reported to Captain Roy Hoffman, a veteran of World War II and Korea whose Navy rank was equal to a full colonel in the Army. Hoffman now told Kerrey and the other SEALs that a new operation called Sea Lord would focus on canals and rivers in southwestern Vietnam.

The Hoffman briefing left Kerrey wondering exactly what they would do other than inspect junks and sampans. The SEAL platoons did not answer directly to Captain Hoffman or other command officers. Instead, the SEAL Team One commanding officer in Coronado directly controlled Team One patrols operating in Vietnam. Kerrey's platoon leader, Lieutenant Tim Wettack of Coffeyville, Kansas, decided where and how the platoon conducted operations. Naval intelligence identified one opportunity twenty miles south of Cam Ranh Bay. Kerrey drove a Jeep through the countryside to Phan Rang for the interrogation of a VC sapper (combat engineer) slightly older than Kerrey, recently captured directly beneath an American guard tower. Alive only because he might provide information, the sapper glared defiantly at interrogators gathered around his bed in a field hospital.

The next day at a Special Forces compound forty miles north of Phan Rang, Kerrey and Wettack learned about some possible targets and split the platoon to do both missions at once. The Phan Rang area, particularly a beach just below some coastal mountains, offered the prospect of finding both VC and North Vietnamese targets, but the mission busted. Despite this and other disappointments, in a memoir thirty-three years later, Kerrey admired how much the South Vietnamese did in those years with so little modern technology of their own.

Soon, Kerrey and Wettack decided to try again. Kerrey's squad would go to Vung Tua, find any other SEAL platoons nearby, and set up an operation if one seemed feasible. Kerrey remembered Vung Tua years later as an idyllic half-moon-bay opening to the mouth of the Mekong River, where American military crowded beautiful beaches to capture a few days of rest and recreation. During his Vung Tua area survey, Kerrey met with Army and Navy intelligence officers, participated in a swift boat operation on the Co Chien River, and then journeyed on to Cat Lo, a small town on Vung Tau Bay, for Operation Market Time.

Officially, Market Time began in mid-March 1965 to prevent North Vietnamese boats and ships from infiltrating the South Vietnamese coast in swift boat supply missions. The Cat Lo commander offered Kerrey and Wettack a sketchy mission with some potential. The VC controlled Thang Phu province—or so local intelligence sources reported. Kerrey and Wettack could have some swift boats, but air and naval gunfire support didn't exist—a take-it-or-leave-it offer, not an order.

When the SEAL platoon discussed whether to take the offer or decline it, one of the more experienced and trusted enlisted men advised against it since their principal South Vietnamese scout was elsewhere. Even so, Kerrey and Wettack decided to go ahead after learning that a high-level VC meeting was to be conducted soon at a village called Thangh Phu. A surveillance flight conducted on the day of the mission revealed no women or children near the rendezvous houses, so Kerrey's swift boat moved up a nearby canal from Cat Lo several hours after sundown on Tuesday, February 25, beaching about half a mile from the VC rendezvous; they moved along dikes abutting high buffalo grass and broad rice fields and past huts of bamboo covered with grass mats toward the village, hoping against hope that the element of surprise was not lost.

The targeted VC disappeared, but a local informer thought they were still nearby. No men at all could be seen, confirming that the SEALs had been compromised. Worse yet, women and children began gathering in the center of the village just before VC gunfire erupted from just behind the civilians—no coincidence. Kerrey and his men defended themselves but were horrified by the number of innocents caught in the cross fire.

Within minutes, Kerrey could hear swift boats approaching in the canal. He signaled them with a small red flashlight and led his men on board in silence. During the brief trip back to Cat Lo, he reflected on the tragedy, which marked his first firefight. Back in Cam Ranh one week later while waiting for Wettack to return from a companion mission, Kerrey learned of yet another possible opportunity, prompted by the surrender of a VC sapper to American Special Forces at Nha Trang, some thirty-seven miles to the north on the coast. An Army colonel there offered a mission targeting the sapper's former colleagues to Kerrey and SEAL Team One since his own Army unit couldn't conduct the operation in time to take full advantage of the intelligence. The information suggested that the targets were the very VC who used women and children for cover in Thang Phu.

Hours later, Kerrey interrogated the informant himself and decided, if possible, to capture the VC instead of killing them. The targets were on an island near Nha Trang; the swift boat dropped Kerrey and the others in rubber boats about a mile seaward of the island on Friday, March 14, one of the darkest nights Kerrey ever experienced. They would land, hide the boats, and climb 350 feet upward. Kerrey kept the informant in front as they moved upward, hoping to catch the VC cadres sleeping; half of them were, but the other half came out of nowhere, attacking at close range.

Kerrey, injured in the initial volley, tied a tourniquet to his leg and gave himself morphine while directing the SEALs' defense and calling in cross fire. Even so, the firefight went on for about half an hour until the VC retreated, leaving the SEALs in silence. Looking down, he could not see the foot and ankle once attached to his right leg. Thanks to the morphine, Kerrey felt no pain at all as a sling lifted him into a medevac helicopter, breaking a finger of his left hand on the way up. He was injured by the very same grenade that struck a nearby medical corpsman in the eye.

The captured VC political cadre provided intelligence that was later considered critical; Kerrey received the Medal of Honor for his service that day and eventually became a U.S. senator from Nebraska. Although Kerrey lost his leg, a reconnaissance team the next day established that the Kerrey team disrupted a major limpeteer attack in which enemy swimmers had hoped to place powerful limpet mines on nearby American boats and ships.

———

Five years after its inception, in December 1972, Phoenix largely ended, although a few elements continued into 1975. Night assassinations became synonymous with Phoenix, justifiably or otherwise. The PRU numbered fewer than 5,000 yet neutralized more VC infrastructure than all other such South Vietnamese units combined.

The PRU operated in small groups—one platoon usually comprised of three squads in each province. This maximized security and allowed them to surprise the VC in operation after operation small enough to avoid major communist buildups and develop independent, largely reliable intelligence sources. Generally, they conducted small-scale operations—hit-and-run missions involving no more than two squads. Despite its original mission, more often than not, the PRU killed rather than captured intended targets.

The year 1970 became the pinnacle of SEAL involvement in Vietnam, with some 250 men in country. The early SEAL impact didn't reflect their low numbers. By the end of 1968, SEAL-directed PRU operations yielded 800 VC killed or captured monthly, many more of the former than the latter.

Orders in late 1970 prohibiting SEAL participation in combat missions surprised no one. Long before that, the rules of engagement became so restrictive that the SEALs simply discontinued operations. Most SEALs returned to Little Creek and Coronado by June 1971.

Critics point out that Phoenix often targeted shadow VC government officials rather than VC or North Vietnamese soldiers, thus arguably violating Geneva Convention provisions protecting civilians in times of war. Others contend that the Geneva Convention provisions simply did not address the type of "subversive political infrastructure" the VC and its predecessors created. Further, Phoenix defenders contend that the VC civilian collaborators didn't qualify for POW status and could not be considered "persons taking no part in hostilities" under Article 3 of the Convention. Despite highly publicized charges of Phoenix atrocities, investigations by the U.S. Congress did not reveal any hard evidence of any atrocities by any SEALs.

During the last years of the war, the North Vietnamese army (NVA) held some sixty-three American prisoners at Son Tay, about twenty-three miles west of Hanoi. The first successfully executed mission to rescue them didn't bring home a single American POW, although as many as 200 North Vietnamese regulars died. Scott Lyon was among the SEALs in that operation. His prior experience in Vietnam and elsewhere was extensive.

Lyon enlisted in the Navy in 1952, fifteen years before his June 1967 deployment to Vietnam as chief of the Fifth Platoon, SEAL Team Two, which replaced the Third Platoon—the first SEAL platoon to see direct action there. On a later deployment, leading some 180 men, Lyon nearly died during a night operation. Lyon and his interpreter met one informer in a small hut. Lyon went out for a smoke some fifty meters away next to a rice paddy. Seconds later, the hut exploded as bullets began to fly. Lyon became one of the first Seal Team Two advisers in Vietnam operating with PRUs. Years later, Lyon characterized Phoenix as a good program, based on his personal experience kidnapping VC leaders for interrogation and in some cases recruiting them for operations against the communists.

His third tour, in October 1968, brought an extraordinary opportunity. Two women informed his PRU adviser that some Americans were being held captive nearby. Lyon called in the Seawolves, Navy crews flying Army VH-18 helicopters, which began operations in June 1967. Now they operated from USS *Harnett County*, an LST-821 landing ship. The plan called for a South Vietnamese army company (Army of the Republic of Vietnam [ARVN]), a platoon of PRUs, and Lyon's squad of SEALs.

The women informants led Lyon's squad at dawn to Con Coc Island on the Bassac River. Lyon released the women some 200 yards away from the target just as first light arrived. When Lyon crept over the edge of an overlooking hill, he saw several VC (only one armed) guarding two small hooches. He sent the PRUs to the left and had his interpreters warn the prisoners to get on the ground.

They killed seven VC and captured several more before liberating some twenty-six prisoners but no Americans. Several POWs kissed their liberators' feet before diving into some old stale C rations. Many of them had been in captivity since the Tet Offensive ten months earlier.

Colonel John A. Dramesi and other prisoners who were being held near the Hoa Lo Prison, nicknamed the Hanoi Hilton, began final preparations for an escape in late April 1969. On May 10, Dramesi and Edwin Atterberry got away, but less than twelve hours later, they returned, dirty and discouraged, to "The Zoo" four miles southwest of the Hanoi Hilton. In the thirty-eight days that followed, the NVA tortured both of them and killed Atterberry. That September, when Ho Chi Minh died, Dramesi began planning to escape again as SEALs began preparing rescue operations. On August 22, 1970, Team Two, 6th Platoon, led by Lieutenant Louis Boink, raided a POW camp, freed some twenty-eight Vietnamese, but found no Americans.

Meanwhile, the North Vietnamese caught Dramesi trying to communicate with other prisoners on May 10, 1970, exactly one year after his attempted escape with Atterberry was thwarted. By Christmas, some forty-seven prisoners at the Hanoi Hilton shared a single small room where they began discussing escape once again with more senior officers. Although POW Colonel Robinson Reisner issued an order four years earlier prohibiting any escape attempt at all without firm assurance of outside assistance, he now asked Dramesi to research, plan, and organize another effort. By February 1971, lack of interest reduced the working group to four men, but they developed a plan. And Navy SEALs became part of their return to freedom.

Dramesi discovered some plastered-over drain holes where they could hide supplies stolen from the North Vietnamese soldiers. That done, they presented their plan to the senior officer in charge: they would escape through the ceiling, as several men did before, carrying plastic bags for use as life preservers and waterproof gear packs. Even though the senior officer turned them down and despite a warning from a friendly North Vietnamese captor that his next escape attempt would be his last, Dramesi continued planning.

This time, the stubborn quartet had some outside assistance. Someone among the local North Vietnamese population provided them with a detailed map of Hanoi, hidden in a hollowed-out piece of wood and delivered through a gutter, even including the most recent World Series scores. Soon, they also had disguises, used mirrors to signal the American forces, and even snagged some snacks.

Despite all this, the senior ranking officer now insisted that the escapers obtain advance permission from American forces. American intelligence operators granted it and designated Dramesi's escape plan Operation Diamond. SR-71 Blackbird planes began reconnaissance as SEALs went on standby status. The crews stationed at Kadena Air Base in Okinawa, 1,433 miles east of Hanoi, nicknamed the SR-71 "Habus"— a reference to a venomous pit viper that had inhabited the area around the airfield for thousands of years. The Habus could fly over Vietnam in eight minutes or less.

A special mission planning board created in 1970 reviewed the feasibility of rescuing POWs held in North Vietnam, identifying the Son Tay camp as the first target. Ground intelligence revealed that as many as sixty-three servicemen were held there in very bad circumstances. Even though the Son Tay raid that November failed, the Americans planned more such missions—one rather mysterious. On May 2 and 4, 1972, three unbriefed Habus crews released sonic booms over Hanoi as a signal to the POWs. Decades later, the crew members learned the purpose of that mission. American prisoners planned to escape from camps near

Hanoi during the first two weeks in June 1972. Whatever their number, they would flee southeast to the Gulf of Tonkin.

Navy Lieutenant Commander Edwin L. Towers soon learned that he would be creating the game plan and selecting the men performing it. He considered Navy SEALs aboard USS *Grayback* (call sign Panther) best qualified for the job. *Grayback* and its sister ship *Growler*, then among the largest submarines in the world, carried Regulus II missiles that could be launched on eight minutes' notice from two hangars. But in the 1960s, the Navy refitted the silent diesel-powered *Grayback* as a special operations transport. Each of the two hangars had a wet side and a dry side, the latter for preparation and maintenance of equipment. The wet side could be flooded to prepare SEAL Delivery Vehicles (SDVs) for launch. The SDVs were miniature submersibles that could be released while *Grayback* operated underwater.

The Thunderhead plan assumed that the escapees would secure small boats on the Gulf of Tonkin and then signal with a red or yellow flag in daytime or red lights at night. The SEALs deployed to survey some fifty miles of the Tonkin coast, including the Red River estuaries and waterways, looking for them.

Back at the Hanoi Hilton, Dramesi planned to follow the Red River once the POWs escaped. Only a handful of the many Navy personnel involved in the operation were fully briefed on all the details. Ongoing air strikes against targets in the Hanoi area would also provide cover for the escape.

Helicopters would search the entire designated area, watching for small craft giving the prearranged signal. Each one-ton SDV Mark VII, MOD 6 ("Six Boat") would be flooded with water, so the driver, navigator, and two fully equipped SEALs had to wear breathing gear. *Grayback* had one additional unique feature that increased the chances that the operation would be entirely covert. Intake outlets on the side rather than on the bottom of the boat allowed release of the SDV from just above or even on the ocean floor.

Alpha Platoon, newly designated as the Special Warfare Western Pacific Detachment, deployed at White Beach on Okinawa to conduct training while preparing for quick-reaction missions. Some of the

SEALs worked as carpenters, building a diving locker and paraloft, a building where parachutes could be inspected, repaired, and packed. These Southeast Asian combat-hardened SEALs trained with UDT units and Philippine Special Operations. They even did some mountain climbing in Korea.

They briefed in—but not on Thunderhead. Instead, Alpha Platoon SEALs learned that their mission involved conducting demolitions in response to North Vietnamese attacks on USS *Buchanan* in which one American died. The SEALs were to attack the responsible enemy artillery batteries at Haiphong Harbor, destroy them, and escape in rubber boats.

They trained by swimming for miles and conducting full-dress nighttime insertions and patrols, while UDT operators practiced launching and recovering the SDVs. Alpha consisted of twelve men and two officers, only a few of whom fully briefed in on the mission. Finally, the SEALs learned that they would launch an SDV at night from the submerged *Grayback*. They planned to establish an observation post and monitor the North Vietnamese coast for red flags or lights from small watercraft sent by Chinese or North Vietnamese defectors. Alpha members conducted many similar missions before. And as *Grayback* approached North Vietnam, the platoon quietly celebrated Philip L. "Moki" Martin's promotion to warrant officer by having some fresh-baked cake.

Thunderhead was so secret that the crew of only one of the seventy ships that *Grayback* passed under knew about their mission. And the *Grayback* crew couldn't even watch movies for fear that the projector noise might reveal their presence, even as HH-3A helicopters above the water began searching for any sign of the escapers.

Grayback settled on the bottom in some eighty feet of water on Saturday, June 3. Few on board knew the mission details. They soon arrived on station near the island, which served as the observation post. Three SDVs carrying SEALs were to rotate onto the island and wait for developments.

The first SDV, launched at 2:00 the next morning, carried newly promoted warrant officer Martin armed with a Swedish K 9-mm submachine gun. The UDT crew consisting of Lieutenant Melvin S. "Spence"

Dry, Tomas Edwards, and John Lutz guided the SDV out against a two-knot current pushing against them from a river outlet. Worse still, they couldn't even see the island due to navigational errors.

Just before daybreak, Towers, aboard USS *Long Beach*, got the message he hoped not to see: *Briar Patch Tango*, the signal for trouble. Towers didn't know that the first SDV deployed in the operation lost all power, but within minutes, a rescue helicopter hovered above the four men on board it. Once the men jumped onto the rescue chopper, the helicopter quickly sank the powerless SDV by machine gun fire. Then the SEALs dropped onto a beach fifty miles from Vietnam for debriefing as others continued the mission. Later that night, Lutz, Edwards, and Martin would be dropped next to *Grayback* at 11:00 p.m.

Precautions for this top-secret operation were extensive. *Grayback* raised its snorkel above the water ever so quickly and signaled search-and-rescue helicopters with an infrared light. And that's when the difficult part began. The technique that was used to minimize detection by the North Vietnamese required the American helicopter pilot to maintain a twenty-knot maximum speed no higher than twenty feet from the water. Mozi Martin, the jumpmaster responsible for manually signaling the crew chief when the chopper was slow and low enough, would be the last man out. The winds were high, and the sky was overcast as the chopper left *Long Beach*. The pilot flew the first pass on instruments, his first such mission ever.

He crisscrossed the last reported *Grayback* position, but the only lights the pilot saw through his infrared goggles came from North Vietnam. Fuel ran low as tailwinds became high enough to affect the instruments. Finally, when a flashing light appeared, the pilot maneuvered into position and ordered the drop. Martin went out last. He counted to three before hitting the water, knowing that this likely was even more dangerous than the usual drop, far above the usual twenty feet at a speed much faster than twenty knots.

Martin found Tomas Edwards a few seconds later, moaning face-down in the water, but Spence Dry didn't show up, and *Grayback* was nowhere to be seen. The lights the pilots saw came not from *Grayback* but from emergency strobes activated by a second SDV crew in the water.

Now two SDV teams floated helplessly in the Gulf of Tonkin, listening to North Vietnamese patrol boats nearby, some 2,000 yards from shore. Several hours later, Spence Dry floated into the group facedown and lifeless. Someone inflated his life vest while they waited to be rescued. Petty Officer Sam Birky from the second group also came up missing.

Martin and Edwards spotted a search-and-rescue helicopter hovering near the surface in the distance rescuing Sam Birky at about 7:00 the next morning.

The second SDV was seriously overweight but had been launched anyway. This hadn't been any secret on *Grayback*, as some of whose crew could hear the sonar device on the distressed SDV pinging loudly. A third SDV mission would be a surface operation using an inflatable rubber boat called a "Z-Bird."

A heated discussion began between the enlisted SEALs assigned to the third mission and some non-SEAL officers aboard *Grayback* who wanted one of their own on the mission. That argument ended in a stalemate as everyone aboard heard a scraping noise, the sound of grappling chains being dragged behind surface boats. The SEALs, led by the remaining Alpha Platoon petty officer, Rick Hetzell, broke out their weapons and prepared for a possible surface mission in which the SEALs would swim to the surface to take on any attack boats in the area. Later that day, *Grayback* sustained friendly fire but survived.

The circumstances of Dry's death remained officially secret until February 5, 2008, when the United States posthumously awarded him the Bronze Star with Valor insignia during a formal ceremony at Annapolis, Maryland.

CHAPTER FOUR

Treasure Trove

THE SURFACE-TO-AIR (SAM) MISSILES DIDN'T APPEAR ON GENE HAM-
bleton's scope but killed everyone behind him in the B-66 Destroyer.
Somehow, he punched out as quickly as the doomed pilot in front signaled Hambleton to bail out. Five or six miles and twenty minutes above
the ground, all too soon he began a slow, flat spin, noticing along the
way that, as he feared, no one else got out that Easter Sunday, April 2,
1972. He began mapping out a plan before falling into the jungle, as he
had been taught in a water survival course at Turkey Run, Florida, and
the Vietnam survival "snake school" at Clark Air Base, Philippines, as
described in the 1989 book *Bat-21* by William C. Anderson.

Hambleton activated the beeper built into his parachute harness,
then bandaged a finger he banged up ejecting, just before he spotted a
forward air controller (FAC) American observer plane far below him.
Somehow he made radio contact, knowing that he could be landing right
in the middle of the NVA. The ground fog below hid the dry rice paddy
he landed in, still wearing the old-man reading glasses he had been using
to read navigational charts before the SAM hit them. His first instinct
after the thud told him to pull in and hide his massive parachute before
the enemy spotted him, but when mortar fire started, he jumped into a
ditch instead. Soon, a helicopter began churning above, but the dense fog
prevented a rescue. Hambleton emptied his survival vest, picked up the
knife kept in one of the pockets, and then dug a foxhole long and wide
enough for him to sleep in, covered by whatever leaves he could find. The

most important lesson from his survival schools: pick out and do at least one task a day to keep your spirits up during what might be a long wait.

Hambleton knew that the artillery attack that brought him to this dangerous place began just after midnight on Friday, March 31, 1972, Good Friday, in the northernmost provinces of South Vietnam. By noon that day, three divisions of Russian-built North Vietnamese tanks all began converging toward Quang Tri City. Only days ago, Iceal G. "Gene" Hambleton, sometimes called Hambone, was anticipating a few days in Bangkok with his wife Gwen. He was fifty-three, far older than most flying reconnaissance missions, but still in harness despite forty-three Korean War combat missions and another sixty-three in Vietnam under his belt.

Hambleton had parachuted out of Bat-21, a clunky old light bomber first flown in June 1954. The RB-66 photo reconnaissance version he had been in carried six men instead of three, sweeping and jamming radar in advance of B-52 bombers and fighters in highly classified missions.

Bat-21 and Bat-22 conducted radar-jamming electronic counter-measures to protect three B-52s bombing NVA troops north of Cam Lo. Bat-21 augered in after dropping the payload. The EB-66s now began diverting Soviet SAMs away from B-52 bombing formations. Once a SAM locked onto an EB-66, the pilot would wait ten seconds and execute a tight diving turn to avoid destruction, but this mission wasn't typical. This time, in the early hours of Sunday morning, the NVA got an extra five-second jump on the Americans by launching the SAM when the contrails of Hambleton's plane became visible rather than waiting for the radar signature. Before the shoot-down, Hambleton served in four distinct jobs, serving as reserve copilot, engineer, navigator, and electronics officer. His job now, on Easter Sunday morning, was survival, surrounded by tens of thousands of NVA regulars. His detailed knowledge of electronic countermeasures equipment, tactics, and strategic missile forces would be highly valuable to the Russians if he were captured.

He awoke at dawn in a makeshift foxhole he dug when he landed to the noise of machinery somewhere nearby. He crept to a hedgerow a few feet away, peeped over it, and saw dozens of Russian-built trucks rumbling south on Highway 561 from North Vietnam at its intersection with Highway 8B, another major thoroughfare. Hambleton somehow landed at a major staging area for the largest North Vietnamese initiative of the war so far. Nearby, among parked trucks, tanks, and heavy guns, some North Vietnamese regulars pointed angrily at something one of them found: his parachute. Within the next few minutes, they all began looking for him.

Hambleton crawled back into the foxhole, keyed his radio, reported developments to the rescue command, and waited for the usual spotter plane to appear. And when it did, he flashed a small mirror three times, just hoping he hadn't been seen by anyone else. Within minutes, a flight of Douglas A-1E "Sandys" began dropping clusters of bomblets the size of lemons called "gravel" around him. He could safely move around within a one-mile perimeter. After confirming the target coordinates, he watched several Sandys destroy the trucks and guns he reported. Several minutes later, F-4 Phantoms began making passes, leaving bodies and burning metal in their wake. The choppers now came clattering and chattering in, barely visible when the North Vietnamese antiaircraft fire from a nearby village opened up, along with assorted small-arms fire to the east. Some of the F-4 Phantoms regrouped to give the choppers cover—but not in time to pick up Hambleton that day.

He spent a second night among enemy soldiers whose patrols came ever closer. Hambleton, just about asleep at 2:00 a.m. on day 3, heard noise coming from nearby. Soon he watched North Vietnamese regulars with flashlights leading villagers through rice paddies looking for him, probably forcing the civilians to pick up the explosives he occasionally heard detonating. About an hour later, the North Vietnamese traffic moving south along Highway 561 resumed, lighted intermittently by flares that could be quickly extinguished when American planes approached again. He quickly called in, arranging for more Phantoms to make yet more strikes. Soon after that, he raided a nearby garden for berries, pineapples, and corn on the cob. Hambleton, dirty, unshaven, and homesick but still alive, knew that by then the North Vietnamese were examining the RB-66 wreckage. In all likelihood, they knew from monitoring radio transmissions that a valuable electronic countermeasure expert might be alive and hiding nearby.

On the morning of Tuesday, April 5, Hambleton hoped for a quick rescue but knew that the Jolly Green Sikorsky HH-3E helicopters couldn't fly the day before due to weather. He didn't know that one of the OV-10 FAC observers crashed in the jungle, costing the pilot his life. The observer, First Lieutenant Mark Clark (no relation to the World War II general of the same name), survived but was on the run. Later, as Hambleton reported from a small knoll that he could see enemy movements, a bedraggled, shabbily dressed ten-year-old with a dirty, gaunt dog appeared. Hambleton played dead as the boy poked him with a stick; the dog sniffed, growled, and bared his teeth, but the boy lost interest, turned back to the village, and walked away, the dog trailing behind him, seemingly oblivious to the deadly minefield beneath them.

Somehow they survived, but now the boy pointed in Hambleton's direction over his shoulder. As three North Vietnamese soldiers approached, he called air rescue more out of desperation than hope. The NVA loomed only about ten feet away when an O-2 FAC appeared from out of nowhere and fired nonlethal rockets to mark the target. Two of the three NVA blew themselves up in the minefield trying to escape. Later, his rescue contact told Hambleton that the choppers would be coming for him the next day. But after dusk, he saw NVA regulars setting up the very type of SAM-2 (S-75 Dvina) missile that brought him down. Hambleton alerted his contact and formulated a plan.

That evening, each time a missile ignited, he warned his contact to have incoming American planes take evasive action. After twenty-five launches, the NVA simply gave up. A brief but heavy rain that night provided drinking water. On Thursday, April 6, an Army colonel explained to the Joint Chiefs of Staff in Washington why Hambleton hadn't been rescued yet.

Just about that time, back in Vietnam, Hambleton dreamed of a squadron clambake he had attended back in the States but awoke at dawn covered only by a mosquito net. What a war, he thought, when he noticed black spots on his right leg and side, caused by the Russian flak that struck the plane.

While he picked the debris out of his infected wounds, the sounds of approaching planes, bombs, and antiaircraft became louder and louder.

Most likely, he thought, the Americans had targeted a bridge several miles to the southwest. The noise brought nearby Vietnamese out of their houses that morning.

Hambleton began considering his limited options if the rescuers didn't show up. Laos, ninety miles to the west, tempted him, knowing the road east to the sea to be completely behind enemy lines and a trip north all but certainly meaning eventual capture. His spirits were lifted a few hours later when a FAC dropped a package to test NVA defenses near his location and only drew small-arms fire. Within minutes, he heard them coming for him, just before a rescue chopper and an escort gunship became visible to the east. His radio contact directed him to a clearing thirty yards from where he hid.

Just before he made the dash, machine gun fire from nearby tore into one of the choppers, turning it into a ball of flames, taking five men to their deaths. Shortly after midnight on April 7 back at the command post monitoring the rescue efforts, two men argued about what they needed to do. Two hours later, Hambleton lie awake wondering what lay ahead when the sound of a small plane above brought him back to reality. He called his contact for a status update but learned only that there would be no ride out that day. And Hambone had no food. He went back to his secret garden for more corn, but while returning to his hiding place, Hambleton was nearly spotted by some VC with flashlights, no doubt searching for him but taking a cigarette break. They came so close that he could see their features, just before the B-52s he had been hoping for arrived, covering everyone with debris. One of the observers flew over him just after the bombers finished and radioed Hambleton that another rescue was being developed. He savored new hopes of escape until one look at the village brought him back to reality. NVA soldiers began pulling mine detectors off a truck.

In the hours that followed, the trackers became relentless, lowering Hambleton's spirits one detonation at a time, until a Hercules C-130, armed with Gatling guns, lumbered into sight with a Sandy on each wing. They didn't fire a shot. Instead, a white blizzard of leaflets fluttered toward earth, even as the VC minesweepers moved ever closer. Saturday, April 7, found Hambleton trying to recover from a night of fireworks that began at sunset while VC soldiers, alerted by the leaflets, intensified efforts to find him quickly. Some seven minesweepers cleared a path through the gravel at least until the main American show began. First, AC-130s dropped overpower flares, so bright that artillery spotters couldn't identify targets. VC minesweepers finished up about midnight, mingling among villagers herding livestock they could coax through the minefields. Hambleton felt a few pangs of guilt, knowing that many of them were leaving their homes for the last time thanks to him.

Things got worse; even though the village was vacant, fog now prevented the Americans from coming back, at least for now. Back at Seventh Air Force headquarters, John Walker requested another Jolly Green helicopter rescue operation into an area that became one of the most active zones in Vietnam. The commanding general who wrote letters of sympathy to the survivors of the five men who died the day before now initially turned Walker down. Walker played his last card, reminding the two-star that Hambleton, a staff officer for the Strategic Air Command, offered a virtual treasure trove of valuable intelligence for the Russians. The general turned Walker down again, but planners now brainstormed the problem from Thailand to Washington and points in between.

Just after midnight on Sunday, Walker's team pored over maps and diagrams, trying to figure out how to rescue Hambleton without another "close-in" helicopter rescue. The Evader flew only two miles south of the Song Cam Lo River. A ten-mile float might bring him to a chopper landing zone. All Hambleton had to do was walk through hundreds of lemon-sized land mines. In the mid-afternoon, one of his radio contacts gave Hambleton the bad news about the chopper disaster the previous day but again promised that a plan was in the works.

At about 1:00 the next morning, the same contact instructed Hambleton to get ready. The go-ahead came just before dawn. Knowing that Hambleton remembered the details of his favorite golf courses, he was told to "tee off" from the first hole at Tucson National Golf Course, which meant walking southeast. Hambleton measured off his steps and then came to a fork in the path he followed. He keyed the radio and got new instructions referencing a specific hole at Augusta National and several other courses. Around dawn, he stumbled over a dead pig as trucks rumbled southward nearby.

He woke up at about noon on Monday, April 10, smelling tea and food wafting out of a nearby hut. Hambleton walked on through the day and then called in twenty minutes after midnight. This time, he got more promises of rescue and instructions to move through territory he had never seen. He snuck up to an abandoned hooch for breakfast—or so he thought. Something flopped out the door, but when Hambleton reached for the chicken, he got a handful of VC instead. The VC slammed right into him, sliding a blade into Hambleton's left shoulder, but when he raised the knife and tried again, Hambleton slid under, stuck his own knife into the VC's midsection, and ran for his life.

At 4:00 that morning, while Hambleton was hiding behind a farmhouse and underneath a slop trough, his worried rescuers decided where to send him next. When they did, he started through some banana trees. There, Hambleton could tap water running from the top of the trees in the darkness. After drinking from four trees, Hambleton slept deeply until nightfall.

The next day, Tuesday, April 11, the rescue team learned that some ten armored personnel carriers now pursued Hambleton, even as the North Vietnamese offensive intensified. Hambleton tripped over some barbed wire in the darkness, momentarily losing and then recovering his radio before trudging on.

Minutes later, he thought he could see the river just ahead, took a few steps, and fell off a cliff. Exhausted though he was, Hambleton clasped his arms around his head, just as he had been trained to do in survival school, eventually rolling into a tree. But at least he saw the riverbank. A quick call to the rescuers with the good news brought more anxiety instead. VC were now right behind him. Although totally exhausted, Hambleton swam the river as quickly as he could. The 200 feet of river in front of him seemed as broad as the Mississippi, but now he could hear the men chasing him. His weapon, survival vest, and first-aid kit couldn't come along for the swim. He shouldn't have kept his boots, either, but realized this only when in the water. Hambleton took them off, waded back in, and promptly fell in a deep hole. Somehow he got to the surface, swam some twenty feet to a shallow spot, and began walking. Since this part of the river contained many sharp rocks, Hambleton soon returned to the shore for his boots. Somehow he got to the other side before VC flashlights illuminated the river.

He called his radio contact in the darkness only to discover there would be no rest, exhausted though he was. Hambleton crept back into the shallows, fighting snags, branches, and more sharp rocks on his way downstream. Suddenly he felt a sharp pain in his back. He had been struck by a charred railroad tie just as he passed a giant mud turtle. He grasped the branches above him to speed the trip along when not pulling leeches off his skin.

Just then, Colonel Andrews, the commanding officer of a Marine detachment, told his Air Force counterparts about the two-man mission preparing to parachute to Hambleton's rescue. He had been shot down eleven days ago.

Hambleton, now barely asleep, saw something half a football field behind him upstream: a large eyeball painted on the prow of the long-boat in the moonlight. Soon six soldiers began carefully inspecting the riverbank with flashlights.

Before he could duck, one of the soldiers poked an oar at his railroad tie and then got out of the boat to look closer. Hambleton, now dug into a hole, watched the VC put his hand on the charred railroad tie, draw it back, and look at his fingers. The other VC in the boat talked a minute, looked back upstream, and pushed off, never knowing that their target watched them from just a few feet away.

At dawn, one of the observers talking to Hambleton by radio landed his O-2 and briefed one of Hambleton's oldest friends, Colonel Frank Ott, on the evader's precarious position.

Colonel Ott thought of Hambleton as a tall, lanky drink of cactus juice. Anything but handsome, his type of tanned, deeply lined face was more often seen on farm tractor drivers than intelligence operators doing complicated mathematical calculations. He was not top-shelf but was competent. More important, Hambleton put mission before personal safety. While waiting to be rescued, he called in numerous enemy move-ments, pinpointing at least three North Vietnamese SAM locations.

They talked options. C-130s could get close enough to take care of the VC and North Vietnamese soldiers, but Hambleton's position likely would be exposed. The Air Force now considered a smaller helicopter air strike followed by an airdrop of food and water in a dozen different places to confuse the enemy.

About twelve hours later, Hambleton woke up again, scanned the river, and stuffed the mosquito net into his flying suit. Three airplanes came out of nowhere and made drops, and then another ten more dropped more packages, one of which landed behind a banana tree on a small hill above him. After three tries, Hambleton realized that he couldn't walk, even for the short trip. Two hours later, his radio contact gave him the good news. Mark Clark was rescued. Hambleton's time was coming.

But on Thursday, April 13, Admiral Moorer, 7,500 miles away from Saigon in the Pentagon, worried. The briefers told him Hambleton didn't have the strength to pick up a canister of food and water that was dropped for him just yards away. He weakened more every minute. "I want that man recovered," Moorer said to no one in particular. Everybody in the room knew what had to be done, but nobody knew how. And the president also wanted reports on their progress.

At dawn, the twenty yards between Hambleton and the rendezvous point downstream seemed like 200. He paddled on as the charred railroad tie beneath him seemed to get heavier and heavier. The last observer gave him only one piece of advice: keep your eyes open, but he couldn't.

Hours later, he dozed on his floating railroad tie when the sound upstream began and soon snapped him back into consciousness. A sampan slid into the bank right next to him before Hambleton could get his knife into position. I'm done for, he thought, before asking himself whether that was an American pushing back banana leaves and rising from the middle of the boat.

"What's your dog's name?" a southerner said just before Hambleton readied himself to stab another VC but now tried to figure out what the hell this guy wanted. Finally the password came to him. "Pierre—his name is Pierre." Tom Norris hesitated but finally whispered a single word.

"Congratulations!"

Later, as they exchanged pleasantries, Hambleton learned about his rescuer's unlikely trip to the Navy SEALs despite being an Eagle Scout and college graduate. The eyesight problems that kept him from becoming a pilot may have been a factor in his mediocre performance during Basic Underwater Demolition/SEAL (BUD/S) training. His instructors considered washing him out, but in the end gave Norris a pass, maybe because of the tenacity that earlier made him a collegiate wrestling champion at the University of Maryland.

Hambleton didn't know the whole story yet, but at least eleven airmen already died, and two more were captured trying to rescue him, losing five aircraft in those missions. The Vietnamese steersman pushed the sampan away from the bank as Hambleton tried to cover himself in the same spot where Norris was hiding seconds earlier. Two Sandys and a flight of Phantoms flew by directly above them. Where is the cavalry? An hour later, Hambleton figured that one out. "We stop here," the steersman whispered, moving them next to the bank under the overhanging bushes, less than a mile from an NVA contingent looking for them.

"Call it in," the South Vietnamese Ranger whispered to Norris—and he wasn't asking. The NVA moved down the river right toward them. "The Blackhats are coming," Norris said almost inaudibly into the radio. White phosphorous soon appeared just in front of the enemy. An F-14 followed, reducing the dense vegetation to ground level. The NVA disappeared.

Minutes later, Norris and his South Vietnamese partner paddled silently as Hambleton rested, but that didn't last long. Yet another NVA patrol appeared on the right bank, waiting to ambush the trio. This time, Norris couldn't raise anyone, but Hambleton's radio worked. Three bomb runs later, the second NVA platoon left, and the sampan began moving. By mid-morning, they dodged increasing sniper fire.

This did not become the short boat trip to a waiting helicopter that Hambleton expected. After crossing a river, they spotted a Russian PT-76 Reconnaissance tank, its barrel pointed right at them. And this time, the NVA waited for the American planes, hoping to destroy every one of them. Twenty minutes later, the tank became a smoldering wreck, but the observer plane overhead took some hits and headed back to base as the trio floated onward.

The next Vietnamese men they saw rescued the Americans. Norris pulled Hambleton to his feet and pointed up a hill, saying they might be captured any second. They could hear small arms in the far distance as Hambleton tried to walk but soon collapsed. One of the South Vietnamese who had just joined them tossed Hambleton over his shoulder and carried him to safety in a cement blockhouse built thirty years earlier by the French. Far too soon, NVA mortar shelling, punctuated by machine gun fire, found them.

Norris bad-mouthed the Air Force in jest before calling them for help but didn't complain at all when silence at last prevailed. An armored personnel carrier clanked into view, someone opened the hatch, and Hambleton was lifted from a litter and stuffed inside. An hour later, he was looking at a helicopter in a clearing.

"Welcome to the clubhouse," said the chopper pilot, as medics started Hambleton on intravenous feeding. Hours later, in the hospital at Da Nang, Hambleton refused a bedpan but accepted a phone call. Admiral Tomas Moorer, Chairman of the Joint Chiefs of Staff, called to ask about his golf game and express his admiration.

Now, Hambleton learned more about the men who had rescued him as well as those who died or were captured trying as well as the details behind his rescue.

First Lieutenant Bill Jankowski, piloting an O-2 Cessna Skymaster forward observation plane, watched two SAMs streak upward past him, then saw the explosion that brought Hambleton down. Seconds later, while steering around the falling wreckage, he heard a beeper, looked up at a parachute several thousand feet above, and made contact with Hambleton on the emergency frequency, then followed him down and plotted his position just east of a village called Cam Lo near a critical bridge. Hambleton had landed smack dab in the middle of the North Vietnamese invasion force on the way south. The Air Force operations center at Korat Royal Thai Air Force Base 160 miles northeast of Bangkok Korat, Thailand, already knew about the downed crewman. Major Dennis Constant quickly gathered his crew and hurried to a plane.

That day, Hambleton wondered why he was being asked to "make like Charlie Tuna" as Andy Anderson and his team at Da Nang began planning to rescue him. Finally, he realized they were telling him to avoid capture like Charlie Tuna did, a cartoon fish then serving as a spokesman for StarKist Tuna. Anderson eventually called Lieutenant Commander Craig Dorman at the Strategic Technical Direct Assistance Team 158 at Saigon. Dorman had been in country less than a week. He graduated from Dartmouth and the Massachusetts Institute of Technology and now facilitated the SEAL turnover to Vietnamese counterparts under way, even as a major battle raged in Quang Tri province, where 30,000 NVA troops pushed the ARVN to the southern banks of the Cam Lo and Cua Viet Rivers. B-52 bombers stopped the NVA advance—temporarily. Norris stayed behind as the most combat experienced SEAL left in Vietnam.

Lieutenant Colonel Andrew E. "Andy" Anderson, attached to MACVSOG subunit MACVSOG 80, developed and implemented plans to rescue downed flyers. Colonel Anderson planned to get on the scoreboard with his first successful mission.

Anderson pitched General Marshall on April 8 in Saigon and then called Dorman, who recalled years later how Anderson described the problem. The North Vietnamese shot down three American airmen. Two of them hid near a river, surrounded by NVA regulars. The rescue team would move upstream from a safe location, find the airmen, and bring them downstream. Anderson needed someone experienced working with the Vietnamese who was good in the water. And, of course, that added up to a Navy SEAL.

Just after the briefing with Dorman and Anderson, Norris was on his way from Saigon to Da Nang by himself in a six-passenger T-39 Sabreliner. He met Anderson at 8:00 p.m. and learned that he would be leading a new recovery squad.

MACVSOG was established eight years earlier to conduct reconnaissance, intelligence, and unconventional operations in Vietnam, Laos, and Cambodia. CIA personnel joined the mission in 1972. At first, Dorman didn't know of anyone in his dwindling American forces to rescue Hambleton. But Navy SEAL Lieutenant Tom Norris, currently training South Vietnamese in sea-commando tactics and serving as their primary American adviser, just happened to be in Dorman's office when the call came in.

The last SEAL platoon left Vietnam the preceding December. Now MACVSOG was downsizing to become STADT 81, which focused on training their Vietnamese replacements. Norris and Dorman were among the last Navy SEALs in Vietnam.

Anderson knew Norris slightly. Fortunately, on his first tour with SEAL Team Two, Norris learned just enough Vietnamese to get by during operations.

Within hours, Norris started for Da Nang. Anderson briefed the small team that night. They would position themselves on the Mieu Giang River and simply wait for Hambleton and Mark Clark, code-named "Nail 38, Bravo," to show up.

Norris didn't think much of the plan but told Lieutenant Vu Ngog Tho, one of the Vietnamese Rangers, what he thought would really go down. Once in the field, they would improvise their own and just tell Anderson what he wanted to hear. Two senior commandos on the team would help Norris manage three less experienced team members.

A briefing just before they left confirmed what Norris and his team already suspected. The NVA now seized as much territory as possible as quickly as possible during the Paris peace talks to leverage Ho Chi Minh's bargaining position. At the same time, ARVN enthusiasm for the conflict began to wane; an infantry battalion positioned a little more than a mile from Clark did nothing to rescue him.

The first stop for Norris and the others was Dong Ha, eight miles from the Vietnamese Demilitarized Zone (DMZ), the northernmost outpost on Route 1. A South Vietnamese counteroffensive on Sunday, April 9, destroyed some forty tanks and killed as many as 1,000 troops, creating a rescue space for the efforts to rescue Clark and Hambleton.

South Vietnamese General Giai was even less impressed than Norris during the briefing he received at 3rd ARVN Division. He told them in broken English that the mission was crazy but agreed to provide transportation and three U.S.-supplied M-48 tanks and a platoon of South Vietnamese Rangers. Norris knew that a random NVA thrust into the rescue area might end in disaster for his team.

The rescue operation outpost bunker, officially called a Tactical Operations Center, three miles west of Dong Ha, occupied a hill overlooking Route 9, halfway between Dong Ha and Cam Lo. The narrow, old French circular bunker, manned by twenty ARVN Rangers and guarded by three M-48 tanks, sported three burned-out Russian T-54 tanks nearby, reminding everyone of what might happen if the NVA discovered them.

No helicopters were coming to help. Bruce Walker and Larry Potts, both shot down on April 7 trying to rescue Hambleton, even then evaded the NVA on foot. Norris started his operation knowing that Walker was too far from the Mieu Giang River to be picked up.

Once in position at Cam Lo, NVA troop movements forced them to move downstream, but from there Norris moved back upstream with a detachment of five looking for Clark. On April 10, Norris started the search, skirting NVA patrols. He even watched an NVA patrol cross Cam Lo Bridge, standing only because it might be needed in the American rescue operation. Norris could go no more than one-third of a mile upstream from the rescue outpost to wait for Clark and Hambleton. He stretched that ordered boundary more than a little, setting up two miles away.

Clark showed up at about 1:00 in the morning on Tuesday, April 11, floating down the river past Norris and his team, oblivious to the noisy six-man NVA patrol that kept Norris from saying anything. By dawn, Norris found Clark hiding near a sunken sampan and eventually convinced him that help had arrived by mentioning the code words "Snake River" and "Idaho" several times.

Back at the bunker, Norris and his South Vietnamese Sea Commandos rested as Andy Anderson prepared Clark for the trip into Dong Ha despite a rocket attack that killed three team members and wounded several more. Luckily, the NVA didn't follow up with a ground attack; the NVA probably thought that they would provoke an air strike by doing so.

Once armored personnel carriers picked up the dead and the wounded for the trip to Dong Ha, Anderson called in an air strike on an NVA column crossing the bridge nearby. The NVA retaliated, targeting the bunker overlooking Cam Lo, catching Anderson, Norris, and the ARVN contingency outside. They dodged artillery rounds, B-40 rockets, and mortars, but one hit Anderson, and several Vietnamese commandos died. After his evacuation to Saigon, Anderson climbed out of a hospital window and hitched a ride with General Winton Marshall back to Da Nang.

On the afternoon of April 10, Norris and his three South Vietnamese commandos carried little ammunition but moved back toward the river, dodging NVA regulars. They watched tank after tank cross the Cam Lo Bridge moving ever closer to their position. That night, Norris led three ARVN Rangers to a position about two miles northwest of the American bunker. In the meantime, Hambleton notified his radio contact that he didn't have the strength to leave his hiding place on the river.

And about then, on the evening of April 11, the three South Vietnamese Sea Commandos began squabbling among themselves. Two wanted to terminate the mission since NVA troops and trucks could be heard only too well, searching for them only yards away. Only Petty Officer Nguyen Van Kiet wanted to see the mission through.

Within hours, the 37th Air Rescue and Recovery Squadron honored the men who had died in the effort to rescue Hambleton. A quarter of a century later, friends, colleagues, and families buried Allen Avery, Peter H. Chapman, John H. Call, William R. Pearson, and Roy D. Prater with full military honors at Arlington National Cemetery.

That Tuesday, April 11, while Norris and his team rested, signs that Hambleton's ten days on the run in the bush were beginning to take a toll increased dramatically. When a survival kit dropped in only 164 feet away, Hambleton stood on a fully exposed sandbar and waved a white handkerchief upward despite being surrounded by NVA regulars. He knew that Clark was rescued. On the evening of April 10, according to Norris, Hambleton moved from his earlier hiding spot to the Mieu Giang River. Walker's path to the river was still blocked by the NVA.

Norris heard all of this on the radio and began planning. He was supposed to stay within 3,200 feet of the concrete bunker but again ignored orders, walking on point in front of his three Vietnamese comrades. They initially planned to patrol next to the river moving west and hope that Hambleton saw them. They moved quietly in fifty-yard increments, avoiding NVA on all patrols. They didn't talk since Norris didn't know much Vietnamese and no one but Kiet knew any English. Hambleton was supposed to be on the north side of the river about half a mile downstream from Cam Lo Bridge, but he was nowhere to be seen under the waning half-moon that lit the north shore.

On the evening of April 12, even as Norris and Kiet prepared to go out again, NVA mortar and rocket attacks on the rescue operations center began again. Later, Norris speculated that only the fear of air strikes kept the NVA from launching an infantry assault. By mid-afternoon, Norris had developed a plan to rescue Hambleton—by sampan. Even though many boats waited for them in deserted villages nearby, Norris requested canoe paddles, some life jackets, and first-aid supplies.

Earlier that afternoon, on April 12, a TV network film crew and reporter arrived with the supplies, confronting Norris, who was wearing nothing but a shirt, just outside the bunker. Norris planned to go back out for Hambleton alone, but Kiet insisted on going with him. Norris concluded that evening that Hambleton must be rescued now or never.

From a distance, the Americans resembled local fishermen, but anyone looking closely could see that Norris was wearing blue jeans. He carried a small red-filtered penlight to occasionally examine the map. They alternated from the north bank to the other side, avoiding NVA soldiers along the way. On April 12, near midnight an hour upstream, they went into a fog bank and soon went past an NVA fueling station.

Six hours upstream, as the fog lifted, they could see Cam Lo Bridge. Hambleton was supposed to be about three miles back downstream. They found Hambleton shortly before dawn the next morning, sitting on a bush about thirty yards above the river. Unlike Clark, Hambleton knew immediately he had been rescued. And now Norris must decide whether to hide until dark or try to get back in the emerging daylight. Deciding on the latter, he and Kiet helped Hambleton lie down on life preservers on board while they covered him with so many large, broad nipa palm leaves that the seriously overloaded sampan traveled with only three inches of portage between them and disaster. There was no air support available yet since the NVA had just begun a rocket attack on the American air base at Da Nang.

An NVA patrol spotted them about twenty minutes after dawn and crashed through the brush along the bank chasing them but never fired. An NVA machine gunner downstream had an even worse day. Instead of waiting for the trio in the sampan to get close enough to ambush, he opened up on Norris, Kiet, and Hambleton so early that Norris called in newly available air support. After taking out the NVA machine gunner, the A-1s dropped smoke canisters that shielded the sampan during the last 500 meters (one-third of a mile) of the float to the rescue outpost. Once they arrived, South Vietnamese Rangers and commandos carried Hambleton up the hill, even as small-arms fire, mortars, and rockets opened up on them from across the river. Years later, Norris learned that one of the pilots who provided air support that day was Lieutenant Denny Sard, one of his oldest Navy friends.

An armored personnel carrier picked up Kiet, Norris, and Hambleton late on the afternoon of April 13. Hambleton started immediately for Da Nang. Later, he said in a press conference that "it was a hell of a price to pay for one life." Back at Dong Ha, the reporter who tried to interview Norris two days earlier finally got a story, even as Vietnamese civilians and ARVN forces clogged Route 1 headed south while the NVA came ever closer. That evening (April 13), Norris and the three South Vietnamese Sea Commandos trekked from Don Ha to Quang Tri City for a debriefing before Norris prepared a new team for a renewed effort. On the advice of Norris, Bruce Walker began moving east at night instead of going to the Mieu Giang River, where the NVA most certainly expected him. Walker crossed Route 1 and was never heard from again. Some sources say that VC sympathizers spotted and reported him. Another version of events reports that VC irregulars killed Walker on the morning of April 18, while another says that Potts ended up in Quang Binh prison.

Norris and Kiet changed into fisherman garb and began rowing a commandeered sampan upstream. Along the way, they pulled into shore only ten yards away from two NVA sleeping in a bunker and passed target after NVA target. They called in a few, but finally, now in a heavy fog bank, they snuck under the bridge at Cam Lo and watched platoon after NVA platoon cross the bridge before turning back toward home. Through sheer luck, on the way downstream Norris and Kiet spotted Hambleton, dazed, weak, but alive, barely hidden in a clump of bushes; they hid him beneath some banana leaves and began the slow, treacherous trip back to the bunker.

Dawn, Wednesday, April 12, brought new problems. Hambleton began talking gibberish just as the trio passed a patrol of North Vietnamese regulars. And the sampan passed an NVA rendezvous point earlier crowded with dozens of tanks but now empty.

Good fortune gave way to danger moments later when an NVA on the north bank behind a machine gun spotted them and opened up, but he was no match for the five A-4 Skyhawks that Norris had called in from USS *Hancock*. A-1 Skyraiders joined the fray, obliterating other NVA positions in the area that Norris had spotted earlier, also providing M47 smoke bombs to mask the Americans in the escaping sampan.

The hapless but seasoned flyboy even drew fire as Kiet and Norris carried him up from the river to safety. But as suddenly as it started, the Bat-21 rescue ended eleven and a half days after Hambleton parachuted to the ground behind enemy lines. Ten men participating directly in or supporting the operation died, and two became POWs. Larry Potts, captured on April 7, reportedly died in a POW camp, but Bruce C. Walker from the same OVIOA Bronco rescue aircraft evaded capture for eleven days before going missing. His fate is still unknown. Was Hambleton worth all this? Navy SEAL Tom Norris told a reporter back in Dong Ha that this wasn't complicated at all. An American was down in enemy territory, and Norris would do it all over again.

CHAPTER FIVE

Escaping Ben Hai

GENERAL VO NGUYEN GIAP KNEW THAT AMERICANS, LONG TIRED OF the war since the 1968 Tet Offensive four years earlier, would not send in ground troops to counter his Easter 1972 initiative. His objective now: Hue City, which six divisions of NVA Regulars attacked from sanctuaries in Laos and Cambodia, supported by Soviet-furnished artillery and armor. *By Honor Bound*, written by Tom Norris, Mike Thornton, and Dick Couch and relied on largely in this chapter, describes how Giap's forces took Dong Ha on April 28 and Quang Tri on May 2. Later, Americans stopped them cold at Hue City.

Tom Norris arrived in Vietnam that very month. On October 25, he traveled from Hue City to Vung Tau, a coastal city fifty miles southeast of Saigon. There, Commodore Dave Schaible told Norris that he needed a joint Vietnamese SEAL (LDND)–American SEAL mission to survey the defenses and enemy disposition north of Cua Vet Naval Base. On paper, this was a South Vietnamese operation, with Norris doing all the heavy lifting. Norris proposed that two American SEALs and three Vietnamese SEALs do the job. Later, during a discussion of the mission, two American SEAL officers assumed that one of them would be on the Cua Viet mission, but Mike Thornton had the experience that Norris was looking for. Thornton, a native of South Carolina and the son of a World War II infantry veteran, was dyslexic, failed his sophomore year in high school, and joined the Navy at the insistence of his father and a juvenile court judge. He became an engine striker (mechanic) but immediately applied for UDT/SEAL training in Class 49 in Coronado, California. Thornton, one of eighteen out of 129 who graduated, became a member of SEAL Team One. By the time of the proposed Cua Viet mission, Thornton conducted numerous joint missions with LDND SEALs who by then had often been fighting for ten years and knew that the American SEALs would be leaving soon.

The operation would begin in the late afternoon on a junk made of concrete, sailing into the South China Sea, either south of Da Nang or north to the DMZ. The squads consisted of six or seven men, including former VC soldiers who switched sides, called "Kit Carson" scouts. The targeted VC fighters and NVA would be captured if possible for intelligence interrogations.

Thornton and Norris wondered why in the world they were tasked to survey Cua Viet Naval Base. One possibility was an assault by Vietnamese marines to recapture Dong Ha. Or the brass might be planning a feint to draw NVA attention while South Vietnamese Rangers attacked elsewhere. Whatever the reason, Thornton trained the rest of their team while Norris planned the mission details.

The U.S. Navy established the Cua Viet base five years earlier to support combat bases at Dong Ha and several installations in Quang Tri province just south of the DMZ. Cua Viet was a makeshift collection of huts and piers on the south bank of the river, opposite North Vietnamese batteries that took potshots at any ships bringing supplies. The meager defenses manning an assortment of machine gun emplacements depended entirely on naval artillery and airpower for support. The main Cua Viet mission before the Easter Offensive was providing a place where supplies and fuel could be offloaded to river craft for transport up the river to Dong Ha and even onto Quang Tri via the Cam Lo and Quang Tri Rivers. And now the NVA in effect controlled both Cua Viet and Dong Ha. Norris, Thornton, and the three Vietnamese LDND SEALs confronted three vital questions. How strong were the NVA fortifications, how many men were there, and, most problematic of all, how seasoned were they?

This would be a single-night reconnaissance operation, hitting the beach at dusk and starting back to Thuan-An by dawn. Norris picked

"Dogsled" Thornton over several other SEALs because of his swimming ability, firefight skills, and ammunition-carrying skills. This would be a fifty-mile, seven-hour trip upriver to carry out a mission similar to several others recently accomplished without any particular difficulties—or so they thought.

Two of the South Vietnamese LDND SEALs were first-rate, but the night before, Lieutenant Quan, who was supposed to lead the mission, banged himself up in a rickshaw accident. His replacement, Lieutenant Thuan, spoke English, had little combat experience, but hoped to make his reputation in this operation. Even though officially Thuan would lead the mission, he wasn't part of the planning; Thuan and the other LDND SEALs would be briefed just before the mission began. Navy ships offshore would provide direction to the team, which would make most of the trip in Vietnamese junks and transfer to an IBS (Inflatable Boat, Small) or paddle onto the beach. The Navy ships would also call in 105-mm howitzer fire support if needed.

Norris rolled out his preliminary plan; called in a patrol order on the afternoon of Monday, October 30; and then briefed Mike Thornton and Bill "Woody" Woodruff, who would serve as the SEAL adviser on one of the Vietnamese junks. The South Vietnamese contingent would learn the details at the last minute to avoid leaks to NVA spies.

Each of the thirty-six-foot Yabuta-class junks used in the Cua Viet operations was made of concrete reinforced with steel mesh and carried a 60-mm mortar, a .50-caliber heavy machine gun, and a .30-caliber medium machine gun. The slow, shallow-drafted Yabuta junks demonstrated remarkable and surprising seaworthiness. The operation began mid-afternoon, paralleling the seacoast, proceeding north toward the mouth of the Cua Viet River. The seven hours, which seemed like fourteen, proved uneventful until just before the "insertion" (SEAL lingo for the landing). One of the two supporting Navy ships left for another mission just before the junks dropped them off—at the wrong river. The Ben Hai River ran miles away from the Cua Viet—and in the middle of the DMZ, not south of it. No one knows to this day whether the American Navy or the South Vietnamese junk captains picked the wrong spot. The SEAL teams initially missed the mistake, absorbed with the details of getting everyone ashore in a three-foot surf, crossing a fifty-yard beach in the open, and getting into some vegetation for concealment.

Within minutes, Thornton conducted a starlight scope survey and discovered that their whereabouts was a complete mystery. They could call the junk crews to come get them, but after some discussion, Norris decided to stay put and look for the target. Thornton's body language indicated he didn't agree, but he said nothing. Norris assumed that after a brief reconnaissance, they might have to return to the junks, spend the next day waiting, and finish the job the following evening.

Tom Norris led the single-file reconnaissance patrol. He was followed by the LDND SEAL radioman, Lieutenant Tuan, and another LDND SEAL, Dogsled Thornton, brought up the rear with a carbine, smoke grenades, the starlight scope, 800 rounds of ammunition, a medical kit, and a life vest. It was 10:30 p.m.

A few minutes into the patrol, they spotted a number of bonfires, indicating that some NVA bivouacked ahead; closer inspection revealed five bunkers, one of which was very large—a permanent NVA base of operations. Norris had moved around or through places like this before on both pilot rescue operations and reconnaissance missions. Even if the NVA spotted them, there might not be any trouble since everyone was relatively small like the enemy, everyone, that is, except Thornton.

They slowly skirted the bunkers moving north but just after midnight saw something on a sand dune about 100 yards ahead. The T-54 tank sported a red star on the turret. Before 3:00 the next morning, they went past the tank, and the NVA crew gathered around a bonfire nearby, going back east toward the beach, hoping to get on the sampans before daylight.

They waded into a creek, going east again, listening to the sounds of the ocean nearby until another noise intruded—the unmistakable voices coming from an NVA encampment that quickly became visible in the far distance. Thornton crept closer and saw that the NVA huts and bunkers offered a clear view of the beach, which Norris and the others would have to cross in the open to escape. Thornton went out again to find a place to hide and stumbled into a foxhole large enough to hide all five of them with their gear. The sandy terrain around their new hiding place reminded Norris of Silver Strand State Beach near Coronado, California, where he had trained for the SEALs. He still didn't know the exact location of their hiding spot.

Fifteen minutes before sunrise, NVA soldiers appeared on the beach, walking toward them. Both NVA would have to be killed or captured. Thornton and Lieutenant Thuan trailed in behind the second man just before Thornton knocked him out with the butt of his stubby CAR-15 rifle. Then Thornton noticed that Thuan let the lead NVA soldier pass without making any effort to kill or capture him. Instead, Thuan simply yelled for the NVA to stop. But when he didn't, Thornton chased him to the nearby tree line and shot him, drawing the attention of an entire enemy squad that chased him until Norris fired a rocket over their heads. And that brought another fifty or so NVA into the fight. Now that daylight arrived, Norris could see that the tank was close enough to the SEALs' position to become real trouble. He called Woody, the SEAL adviser, back on the sampan and ordered some fire support, but nothing happened.

USS *Newport News*, which had been ordered to go elsewhere the prior evening after the insertion, now returned to help. USS *Morton* fired white phosphorous spotting rounds to the predesignated coordinates near Cua Viet Naval Base since no one at all in the operations knew where the insertion team was dropped.

Thornton later recalled that even though the NVA outnumbered them ten to one, the team enjoyed some advantages, several not altogether obvious. First, the NVA did not know that the team was spread out behind the dune to seem larger than it was. Second, the unseasoned NVA troops remained stationary, becoming easy head-shot targets the second time they popped up from behind the same position. More seasoned troops likely occupied ground to the west of Quang Tri City.

During the initial firefight, one of the Vietnamese SEALs interrogated an NVA prisoner who initially refused to say anything. Eventually, the prisoner pointed to their locations just south of the Ben Hai River, ten miles north of the SEALs' assumed location. The race between NVA reinforcements and the Navy artillery support ships would decide whether the SEALs of Ben Hai would survive. Back on the junk, Woody sent an emergency call asking USS *Morton* to begin shooting "spotting" rounds toward the new targets so that the SEALs could call in more precise instructions. Thornton was already through half his ammunition when the grenade-tossing competition began.

A chemically timed Chinese grenade sailed over his sand dune, landing a few feet away. Thornton tossed it back, but so did the NVA soldier. Thornton rolled into a ball, took four pieces of shrapnel in the back, and then watched four NVA charge over the dune; a quicker shot than any of them, he made his count thirty-four for the day. This gave the rest of the NVA on the backside of the hill something to think about for those next critical minutes.

The SEALs hoped that artillery would now take care of the problem, but instead they watched NVA soldiers jump out of several trucks about half a mile down the beach by a shallow lagoon. However inexperienced, the NVA knew enough to split into two groups for the new assault. The dune occupied now by the SEALs would soon become indefensible, but another dune now glimmered in the early morning light some 400 yards to the north. Instead of the textbook leapfrogging maneuver normally used in such situations, Norris sent Thornton and two of the Vietnamese toward the new dune while Norris and the remaining Vietnamese SEALs provided cover from the original position. Norris realized there were simply too many NVA for this to work just as white phosphorous marking rounds began dropping among the enemy soldiers—just in time.

Offshore and unaware of this, Woody monitored traffic and relayed messages while waiting to retrieve the team—*if* they could get off the beach. Worse still, they didn't have the team's exact location. Ideally, Norris and Thornton would send precise targeting coordinates to USS *Morton*; the gunfire support team on board could then use a circular slide rule, called a grid spot converter, to bring the rounds in on the enemy. Woody wondered where precisely the team was hiding. All he could do was pass messages along to *Morton* for Norris, still too far from Ben Hai to do any effective artillery spotting.

Back on the beach, the NVA closed in while the fire team on USS *Morton* waited for the precise information they needed to be of any help. Norris knew only that they were somewhere south of the Ben Hai

River. By the time Norris and Deng moved to the new sand dune, *Morton* moved close enough for Norris to talk directly to the fire team on board. His new best friend was Lieutenant Ed Moore, the relief gunnery liaison. Moore began his shift that morning "walking" spotting rounds north up the coast until, at long last, Norris reported that he could see the fifth explosion. Instead of sending more precise instructions, one of the SEALs yelled, "Shoot, just shoot!" into the microphone. Back on *Morton*, Moore also ignored the usual protocols requiring that he get permission from the captain. Instead, he ordered the gunnery plotters to fire ten rounds.

Instead of the thanks he expected to hear, the radio went silent for a full hour. Moore began trying to call the SEALs on the radio every five minutes but heard nothing. After the war, Moore assumed for years that Norris and the rest of his team were overrun or maybe even killed by the incoming rounds that Moore delivered. Forty-two years later, Moore learned what really happened that day.

Although he didn't know it for four decades, Moore saved the day. Norris recalled later that he was preparing out of desperation to fire his last rocket and start running for the next dune when that spotting round landed among the NVA troops coming for him. Thornton remembered being on the radio there just before an AK-47 round caught up with Norris, hitting him in his left eye socket and exposing his brain. Deng saw him go down, ran for the dune where everyone else was setting up new defenses, and reported that Norris was dead, two hours after the fighting began. The right tactical decision was to leave Norris where he lay and concentrate on setting up the best defensible position on the sand dune. Instead, Thornton ran back to the bunker where Norris lay, past dozens of NVA bodies, even as he watched enemy soldiers silently begin to flank them.

Thornton killed two NVA just feet away from Norris and then did an assessment. Norris sure looked dead, but Thornton picked him up and began running, taking along an AK-47. Ten steps later, a friendly artillery round lifted them both in the air, knocking Norris off Thornton's shoulder and into the sand. Thornton didn't even hear it coming and said later that if part of the dune hadn't shielded them, both he and Norris might have died that morning.

When Thornton began to pick up Norris that second time, Thornton thought he heard something. Just before passing out, Norris, barely audible, told Thornton that he could run but couldn't see. While rounds fell around them, Thornton started for the new makeshift bunker again, holding Norris as steady as possible in a fireman's carry, as friendly artillery kicked up the beach sand around them. Although an Air Force observer above them in an OC-10 Bronco tried to help, he couldn't see much. Somehow, Thornton got back to the new sand dune, even as new NVA units began deploying on the beach, outflanking them. Lieutenant Thuan, the nominal team commander, was nowhere to be seen, but the two enlisted Vietnamese SEALs, Deng and Quan, provided cover fire for Thornton and Norris even though Deng was wounded.

Escaping alive might not be easy. Survival meant dodging friendly artillery rounds and NVA gunfire, running to a beach two and a half football fields away, and hoping that a rubber boat could pick them up—in broad daylight. No one had enough ammunition, but they began to leapfrog away from their sand dune with Norris covering Thornton's back, dropping every thirty-five yards or so to fire single shots at the NVA trying to stop them. Somehow, Thornton held on to the AK-47 that Norris carried and began using it when his own AR-15 ran empty. That happened just after they reached the water. It was time to swim for their lives.

Norris, now barely conscious, could hear AK-47 rounds hitting the water, his vision limited to one eye. Once they passed the breakers, Thornton put his own life vest on Norris, not knowing that Norris had tied his own life vest to his leg. Thornton now pushed and dragged all three of them farther and farther out to sea, amid gunfire that gradually faded away.

All they could do was swim deeper into the ocean and hope someone might see them while Thornton kept them swimming. Their last radio contact with the Navy had been an hour earlier. Back on their junk, Woody wouldn't give up on the team. He pushed the skipper to move inshore between the Navy artillery rounds coming from behind them and occasional Russian RPG-2 antitank projectiles arcing outward from the shore.

Lieutenant Thuan appeared 1,000 yards out from the beach at about 10:30 that morning, bobbing in the water. When Woody asked Thuan what happened to his men, he reported that Norris was killed; Thornton went back for Norris and never returned. Thuan also claimed that Quan and Deng followed him into the water; skeptical, Woody passed this report on to USS *Morton* anyway. When the admiral boarded *Newport News* and learned this, he ordered his ship southward to Quang Tri City, leaving *Morton* to sort out the details. That morning, Commander Schaible, who ordered the mission, considered Thornton and Norris probably dead.

Woody continued the two junk search missions just offshore as Thornton kept swimming, dragging Quan and Norris behind him. Thornton could see the Navy ships from time to time from the crests of swells, but when Deng asked him about the plan, he didn't answer. Yet somehow Thornton knew that Bill "Woody" Woodruff would never leave them behind.

Just as *Newport News* began moving south to support American forces at Quang Tri City, Woody's second junk skipper reported at 11:30 a.m., from about half a mile north and closer to the shore, that he had spotted swimmers in the water.

Norris was unconscious, Quan was just holding on, but Thornton and Deng began yelling and waving when the first junk hove into view and didn't stop until everyone in the water climbed on board. Everyone except Thornton assumed Norris to be dead.

Since he knew that USS *Morton* had no doctor, Thornton and Woody asked *Newport News* to come back, which it did; the thirty-six-foot Yabuta junks pulled up to the 717-foot heavy cruiser, next to the number 3 turret on the port side. Once Peng and Thuan made their way up a ladder to the *Newport News* deck, crew members pulled Quan up on a looped line and Norris in a litter basket.

Only a month before, on October 1, a defective detonating fuse caused an explosion in the number 2 turret of *Newport News*, killing nineteen seamen and wounding another sixty-two. Now, on the last day of that month, *Newport News* doctor Lieutenant Greg Fulchiero and his team immediately went to work on Norris, who soon left for Da Nang and then on to Clark Air Force Base in the Philippines for neurosurgery. Nothing could be done to save Norris's left eye; he asked only if his injury meant the end of his career with the SEALs.

Eighteen months later, Norris retired from the U.S. Navy just after receiving the Congressional Medal of Honor from President Nixon for saving the life of another Medal of Honor recipient.

CHAPTER SIX

In the Shadows

A SEAL TEAM MEMBER IS ONE EXPENSIVE WARRIOR. IN MODERN DOL-lars, a U.S. Marine can be trained for $25,000, but SEAL training for combat costs half a million. Elite DEVGRU SEALs rotate through several regular teams and frogman and hostile rescue training, totaling as much as $2.5 million per year all in. Hell Week now consists of five and a half days of nonstop physical exertion and sleep deprivation designed to weed out all but the fittest. Only about 20 percent survive.

DEVGRU is an acronym created by the United States Naval Special Warfare Development Group that originated in SEAL Team Six. Famed SEAL Richard Marcinko created Six in the days following the disastrous effort to rescue fifty-two American hostages from Iran. In Operation Eagle Claw, eight Americans died when an American helicopter and a fuel transport aircraft collided on the night of April 24, 1980.

Marcinko, tasked to create a new SEAL team within a larger task force being formed to counter terrorist operations against the United States or its citizens, simply edited the first draft to make the task force "all SEAL." Marcinko simply whited out "element" and substituted "command," transforming two platoons into a much larger force of as many as sixteen-man platoons before passing the paperwork up the chain of command. Then he began writing a proposal for a new SEAL unit specifically trained to fight terrorists in a maritime environment. Four days later, Admiral Crowe told him to send it on under a "close hold" secret designation.

Marcinko began working out budget and operational details with SEAL Team Two senior chiefs in Little Creek. Eventually, the first SEAL Team Six ammunition budget was bigger than that of the Marine Corps. After turning down a career-enhancing year at the National War College at Fort Lesley McNair in Washington, D.C., he became first commanding officer of SEAL Team Six and started recruiting the best shooters available.

Adjoining buildings used earlier for Cub Scout functions but resembling chicken coops served as the first SEAL headquarters. One man died in a parachute accident during the first training cycle that November, but now they began testing U.S. reaction abilities in exercises, called full-mission profiles. One involved Puerto Rican terrorists who destroyed a number of planes and stole a nuclear device. In others, they assaulted oil rigs from Denmark to the Gulf of Mexico, freed "hostages," and eliminated terrorists.

Their first hot assignment at the remote southern Caribbean island of Grenada in October 1982 began about ninety days after Marcinko left DEVGRU for another assignment. Cubans and Russians were welcomed to the island months before. Now, Cubans were improving the airfield there to accommodate Cuban and Russian planes or, as Prime Minister Mavrice Bishop claimed, to promote tourism. When hard-liners led by Deputy Prime Minister Bernard Coard ordered Bishop murdered on Thursday, October 19, and imposed a twenty-four-hour curfew, concern began to grow for Americans on the island, most of them students at St. George's Medical School.

The plan called for eight SEALs to be inserted with two Boston Whalers. They began planning insertion of a four-man Air Force Combat Controller Team onshore to manage air traffic control for the invading combat force, but bad luck plagued the operation. The SEALs were supposed to be dropped into the water during daylight, but navigational errors and other problems resulted in a nighttime drop at the wrong location in a sudden squall, resulting in four drowned SEALs and a lost boat. The surviving four SEALs rallied, contacted the destroyer over the horizon carrying the Combat Controller Team, and went on, pushing their surviving Boston Whaler toward the Grenada coast, overloaded with men, supplies, and equipment. The motor quit, forcing them back to the destroyer. A third effort on the night of October 24–25 also failed.

Marines landed at daylight on October 25, but another important mission was assigned to DEVGRU. They were tasked to seize the Grenadian radio station facilities while simultaneously rescuing Governor-General Sir Paul Scoon and his staff at St. George's, the capital. The plan also called for SEAL Team Six teams to quickly assault the governor's mansion and finish the mission within two hours. On Radio Free Grenada, a 75,000-watt station built from Soviet materials to spread propaganda across the Caribbean, government-sponsored broadcasters urged their countrymen to repel the Americans during the early hours of October 25, but the station went silent at about 7:00 that morning. The primary DEVGRU objective was keeping the station intact for later American use, but heavily armored Grenadian forces arrived, forcing the lightly armed SEALs to destroy the radio transmitter and withdraw.

The night-mission rescue of Sir Paul Scoon, presenting a more complex problem, now became as high a priority as rescuing Americans. Once again, delays until just before dawn seriously added to the risk. The Scoon rescue—not exactly a surprise—drew Grenadian artillery, forcing the SEALs to "fast rope" down near the governor's mansion. The SEALs' main radio was seriously damaged; despite this, the second chopper dropped another dozen SEALs onto the lawn, where they fought their way past a "Welcome U.S. Marines" sign and into the mansion.

The twenty-six DEVGRU fighters stuck the governor in a locked closet and established interlocking fields of fire against incoming Cuban forces as a roaming SEAL sniper on the upper floors went from window to window, taking out as many as twenty-one People's Revolutionary Armed Forces (PRAF) fighters. Finally, the Grenadian commander called in armored personnel carriers and other reinforcements.

Since their radio didn't work, the SEALs used the local telephone service to relay their situation to Vice Admiral Joseph Metcalf, who sent in two AH-IT Sea Cobra helicopter gunships to provide air cover early that afternoon. The first helicopter, severely damaged by Cuban antiaircraft fire, managed to crash-land on a nearby soccer field. Grenadians blew a second Cobra, providing fire cover for a medevac chopper trying to reach the first chopper crew at the soccer field, out of the sky, costing two Marine pilots their lives. Thinking he now had the upper hand, the Grenadian PRAF commander ordered an attack on the mansion just as an AC-130 Spectre gunship appeared, destroying one armored personnel carrier and keeping the rest of the Grenadians at bay through the night.

This was clearly not the cakewalk that the State Department had promised Captain Frank Gormly, who followed Richard Marcinko as commanding officer of SEAL Team Six. Gormly recalled years later that the State Department's assumptions that the Cubans would stay in their barracks during the American action was simply wrong. Virtually all of the Cubans in Grenada were combat veterans of fighting in Angola some eight years earlier. The Cubans brought in antiaircraft guns and propped up Grenadian troops, who often put their hands up unless accompanied by Cubans. Later, Gormly commanded SEAL Team Six during the *Achille Lauro* operation against terrorists of the Palestine Liberation Organization (PLO). But now, on the night of October 25, Admiral Metcalf ordered Marine Company Golf to land at St. George's and relieve the DEVGRU Seals at the governor's mansion. The amphibious landing site would be at Grand Mal Bay, just north of St. George's. The Fox Company of Marines landed nearby that Wednesday morning. The combined force, reinforced by five tanks, started immediately for the target. They arrived at the mansion just after dawn and quickly destroyed one of the armored personnel carriers, strongly encouraging the PRAF commander to go elsewhere.

Within minutes, the SEALs, the governor, and his staff evacuated to USS *Guam*.

Perhaps the most unusual SEAL Team Six operation in American history began on the *Achille Lauro*, an Italian luxury liner that docked in Alexandria, Egypt, on the morning of Monday, October 7, 1985. While most of the passengers toured local attractions, four men, Ahmad Marroux al-Assadi, Bassam al-Asker, Ibrahim Fatayer Abdelatif, and Youssef Majed al-Molqi, carrying grenades, pistols, and AK-47s, burst into the ship's dining room.

The terrorists separated eighty passengers by nationality and then moved the American and British passengers to the deck and surrounded them with oil drums. The terrorist destination was Tartus, Syria, a brief cruise away. President Reagan quickly dispatched SEAL Team Six and elements of Delta Force to Sicily, while the Italians and British alerted their own commandos.

Thanks to prior cross-training, the Italian COMSVB and British methods and operations were well known to the SEALs. The terrorist demands surprised no one. They wanted fifty Palestinians held by the Israeli government released immediately. When negotiations broke down, the terrorists quickly picked Leon Klinghoffer, a paralyzed Jew in a wheelchair, for retaliation. The brave terrorists shot the unarmed, helpless sixty-nine-year-old in the head and then forced a waiter and the ship barber to throw Klinghoffer and his wheelchair overboard.

Since Syria refused permission for the ship to dock in Tartus, the *Achille Lauro* cruised on to Port Said, Egypt, arriving Wednesday morning; SEAL Team Six waited for darkness on the *Iwo Jima*, an amphibious assault ship. Using small, silent boats, they would board *Achille Lauro*, kill the terrorists, and quietly leave their Italian comrades in charge to bask in the glory.

Yasser Arafat had a different plan. He loudly intervened, sending PLO emissaries to negotiate a peaceful resolution. His lead representative, Abbu Abbas, a high-ranking PLO official, carried safe-passage guarantees for Egyptian President Hosni Mubarak. The negotiators "convinced" the terrorists to accept Egypt's offer, but the Americans planned something special.

National Security Council counterterrorism expert Oliver North suggested that the terrorists be captured, and President Reagan agreed. The terrorists boarded an Egyptian Boeing 737 on Tuesday, October 10, fully expecting a quick trip to Tunisia, but both Tunisia and Libya denied the plane landing rights. When the 737 turned toward Athens, the F-14 Tomcat fighters from USS *Saratoga* tracking the flight surrounded the 737. The Americans ordered the pilots to land at the NATO air base outside of Sigonella, Italy, even as all other radio communication from the 737 stopped.

SEAL Team Six waited nearby. The United States didn't tell the Italian air traffic controller about the planned reroute until the planes positioned themselves over the country. The SEALs surrounded the plane, but airport carabinieri surrounded them and demanded the right to accept the terrorists' surrender. The SEALs initially considered firing on the carabinieri since they didn't have orders to stand down before Secretary of State George Shultz insisted that the Italians try the terrorists for murder. One is still in prison.

Howard Wasdin had been a SEAL sniper for less than a year in October 1993 when he helped find and capture warlord Mohamed Farrah Aidid, leader of the Habar Gidir clan, one of two factions fighting for control of Somalia, after the dictator Mohamed Siad Barre abdicated under threat of force in January 1991. Some 20,000 Somalians died violently in thirty-four months of turmoil, eventually prompting the United Nations to adopt Resolution 794 and launch a humanitarian relief effort. President George H. W. Bush launched Operation Restore Hope in early December 1992.

Six months later, an Aidid faction mob surrounded and slaughtered some twenty-three Pakistani troops serving as UN peacekeepers. When four American peacekeepers were killed on August 8, 1993, President Clinton approved a Joint Special Operations Command (JSOC) plan to conduct Operation Gothic Serpent, using a task force comprised of Delta Force, Rangers, and SEAL Team Six operators. The SEALs reported to the team command for radio encryption, weapons test firing, and instruction in basic Somalian phrases, such as "hurry" and "stop." Command ordered them to grow long hair and beards. A Ranger ordered them to get rid of all the hair and beards just before they boarded a G5A Galaxy cargo plane at Fort Bragg for the eighteen-hour ride to Mogadishu on August 27, 1993, a Friday. When the team reported to the Joint Operations Center, guarded by troops from Italy, New Zealand, Romania, and even Russia, they noticed that the lopsided roof was covered with antennas.

General William F. Garrison took one look at the SEALs, asked why they didn't have long hair and beards, shook his head, and described the mission. After meetings with the CIA operatives they would be protecting, the four SEALs loaded gear for the operation, including AT-4 antitank weapons, tear gas grenades and fragmentation grenades, and an SST-181 beacon for aircraft coordination. All 160 men slept in an airplane hangar under mosquito nets, while bats dive-bombed the floor, picking up supersize rats for dinner up in the rafters. After three mortar rounds landed nearby, it was lights-out time.

The sun glared as they jumped into helicopters early the next morning for liftoff to who knew where. This was a scouting mission to spot possible routes back from the safe house that was preselected courtesy of the U.S. Army. Most major structures in Mogadishu had been leveled or seriously damaged. Burnt-out cars usually surrounded those few structures still standing. The safe house was code-named "Pasha," the title given to high officials in the old Ottoman Empire. The SEALs scouted landing zones between the safe house and prospective escape routes to the ocean as well as possible boat extraction points. After setting up the safe house and preparing a mosaic map of the area, Wasdin and his crew wisecracked about how this might have been a perfect tourist destination—except for the war. Wasdin later described what happened next in *SEAL Team Six*, a memoir written with Stephen Templin.

Their first stop the next morning, Sunday, August 29, was the Somalia National Soccer Field, some three miles northwest of the Airport Command Center. Battle-worn Mogadiscio Stadium, maximum capacity 35,000, was occupied by Pakistani troops supporting the UN mission. The SEALs and other advance team members jumped onto two dilapidated trucks and used a third as a decoy for the trip into town. They drove through trash barrel fires fueled by animal waste, young boys strutting along with AK-47s, and streets flowing with raw sewage, which also served as the cholera-infested water supply.

Pasha was only half a mile from the stadium. Once a wealthy doctor and his family lived in the two-story structure surrounded by a concrete wall. Now it was a perfect target for robbers—if they could get over the broken bottles along the wall surrounding the property. Despite its size, the house didn't have pressurized running water. Instead, foul domestic water came from a holding tank on the roof. Despite the lack of furniture, they lived like kings instead of SEALs during the first part of the mission, drinking bottled water. Their Somalian chef prepared Islamic-conforming foods, from porridge to pasta, goat to camel, all spiced with cloves, cinnamon, or sage. The SEALs paid the chef using hundred-dollar bills they had been given for escape and evasion.

Local informers ("assets") were briefed and well trained before the SEALs arrived. An asset would deviate from his prearranged route into Pasha if he were being followed and then pause once at a nearby corner if followed by a single individual or twice if followed by two men. Informers arriving at night wore infrared strobe lights.

Signal intelligence operatives assembled monitors and control panels that made their part of Pasha look like a NASA control room, complete with a large collection of roof antennas. A mosaic map of Mogadishu covered an entire wall, marking locations of possible threats as well as the location of Somali warlord Mohamed Farrah Aidid and officer barracks. When the Tactical Operations Center back at the Mogadishu airport was targeted in a series of mortar attacks, the Pasha operators made plans to destroy all the encrypted equipment if necessary.

Even so, the search for Aidid continued. On the last day of August, the SEALs spotted him in a car and began planning a snatch. Aidid reportedly lived near the safe house with relatives. Wasdin and other members of his team had almost grown back their full beards by then, so they began running a reconnaissance patrol in a beat-up old Jeep Cherokee, dressed as locals. Wasdin, dark skinned to begin with, sported a flowery Somali shirt and a man's skirt called a Macawi, with trousers underneath; they all carried SIG 226 9-mm pistols, extra ammunition, and CAR-15 assault rifles stuffed between the seats. Even though they also carried large UDT tactical automatic knives resembling large switchblades, they traveled light by SEAL standards. After finding a prospective helicopter landing zone and a staging area for Delta operators, they came on an abandoned camel slaughterhouse on the beach where fresh replacement SEALs could meet them later. Camel parts thrown into the ocean attracted hundreds of sharks to an otherwise beautiful idyllic beach. On the other hand, since the massive slaughterhouse blocked the ocean view from Mogadishu, it was a perfect SEAL insertion point where Zodiac rubber boats could be paddled ashore in the dark. That night back at Pasha, the SEALs solved a mystery. The team at Pasha wondered how Aidid's warriors had gotten their hands on the incoming rounds landing around the Americans despite constant American air surveillance. During the patrol, Wasdin photographed two colorfully dressed women talking as they carried two babies. Microscopic examination later revealed that one of the women cooed to several mortar rounds instead of an infant.

The intelligence crew intercepted chatter on September 1, a Wednesday, revealing that an attack would soon begin at Mogadishu airport. They notified the Tactical Operations Center just before eight mortar rounds arrived. The break on Aidid they were hoping for arrived the next day thanks to his daughter. She mentioned Aidid's location to a friend during a cell phone conversation, but the ORION P-3 plane tracking him from above lost the trail when the warlord's convoy entered a large building complex.

Air surveillance reinforcements arrived later that day from Europe, even as Aidid began recruiting neighborhood Somalians to report what the SEALs were doing. Instead, many of the Somalians informed on Aidid, as he began accepting help from al-Qaeda and the PLO. Soon, high-level al-Qaeda operatives taught Aidid's militia how to attack American helicopters with rocket-propelled grenades (RPGs) from foxholes to avoid easy detection and supplied other weapons. The Aidid militia killed five to seven Nigerian peacekeepers on the afternoon of September 4 even as mortar rounds fell closer and closer to the SEALs' safe house.

"Leopard," the CIA officer in charge of all Mogadishu operations, was ambushed and nearly killed on the morning of Sunday, September 5. After receiving twenty-five pints of blood, Leopard was flown out to Germany. That very evening, a local informer told the Americans at Pasha that Aidid was visiting an aunt nearby and even provided a diagram of the house's interior, but the SEAL request to conduct an overnight assault was denied without any explanation. Two mornings later, Wasdin and the others heard the unmistakable sounds of a Russian tank approaching the safe house; within hours, Somalian authorities killed two informers. Italians secretly helping Aidid nearly beat a third informer to death. Delta Force captured seventeen Aidid militiamen that evening in the abandoned Russian compound, but Aidid himself couldn't be found. He was elsewhere, coordinating missions against rival Somalian factions, and by September 9, the SEALs learned from their own informers that Aidid knew their location. The efforts to find and capture Aidid continued, but on September 11, SEALs abandoned their Pasha safe house; they returned to the airport and began planning yet another operation, more frustrated than ever.

———

The SEALs next targeted Osman Oli Atto, a fifty-three-year-old Somalian who had managed an American oil company. He also imported khat, a flowering plant from the Horn of Africa chewed like tobacco or boiled as tea in Africa and the Arabian Peninsula. More important, he was second in command to Aidid, whose militia Atto supplied with arms and material. Wasdin started the Atto operation by conducting surveillance on September 13 from a tower near Atto's residential compound. From there, the SEALs could see an open-air vehicle repair garage. Bulldozers and pickup trucks by the dozens being fitted with .50-caliber machine guns on tripods roamed about. These vehicles were called "technicals" since they were unwittingly financed by well-meaning nongovernmental organizations (NGOs) that intended to fund technical assistance. Instead, Aidid and his allies used these vehicles against the Americans and other peacekeepers. Soon after that, the SEALs suggested and received approval to conduct sniper operations on Quick Reaction Force (QRF) helicopter flights over Mogadishu while the hunt for Atto continued.

After several false alarms, Wasdin and several other SEALs resumed their tower surveillance on Monday, September 18, watching for a predetermined signal, distracted by refugee campfires burning in the upper stories of abandoned buildings all over Mogadishu. The informant inside the Atto compound might earn $5,000 by walking into the middle of Atto's garage compound, removing his hat, and walking slowly around. Wasdin spotted Atto wearing his trademarked shit-eating grin just before the informant dramatically gave the $5,000 signal. Seconds later, A MH-6 Little Bird and Black Hawk helicopters arrived on the scene, followed by Delta Rangers fast-roping into the compound.

Wasdin covered half of the open-air garage from a six-story-high tower, soon spotting an Aidid militiaman firing at the Black Hawks from a window 500 yards away and another firing at Delta operators from a fire escape door 200 yards closer. After dispatching both militiamen, he took out a third man trying to fire a grenade launcher above, 846 yards from Wasdin, in the longest shot of his career, but Aidid slipped away through a back door. Early the next morning, Wasdin called in yet another air strike, only to look down at a woman on the ground beneath the tower glaring up, dramatically running an index finger across her throat. Within minutes, Wasdin left for the operations center back at Mogadishu airport.

Delta Force captured Atto the next day thanks to "Honest Abe," the SEALs' favorite Mogadishu informant. Abe made an arrangement through an intermediary to hand Atto an ivory-handled cane—not just any ivory-handled cane but one built around a CIA-constructed homing beacon. Within hours, Delta Force operators called Wasdin, asking him to walk across the operations center to meet someone. The man he met shook with fear. Wasdin's partner, code-named "Casanova," told the interpreter to have the captive smile, but the captive understood English and grinned immediately. Osman Oli Atto, relieved to be captured rather than killed, surrendered with a smile on his face.

While waiting for further orders in late September, Wasdin and the other SEAL Team Six operators began efforts to refine the operations and better coordinate with the Delta team. Team Six Commander Eric Olson helped reestablish SEAL sniper flights with the QRF, now called "Eyes over Mogadishu." As the days crawled by, Team Six went hunting, practiced first-aid techniques, and played volleyball.

Tragedy struck on the evening of September 25, when an Aidid militia member shot down a QRF helicopter patrolling over Mogadishu. While the helicopter crew escaped into the darkness, the Aidid militia mutilated the bodies of three American soldiers who had died in the crash. Pakistani and United Arab Emirate forces protected the surviving American pilots while American military leadership pondered what to do next.

Team Six stood by for hours waiting for rescue mission orders that never came. After a September 28 memorial service in the 10th Mountain Division hangar for the three crash victims, sources told them that problems with Italy and the United Nations prevented the Americans from launching a mission to rescue the two survivors. While waiting, Team Six picked up a new secondary mission: kidnap or kill Aidid militia lieutenant Abdi "Qeybdid" Hassan Awale, known as "Mad Abdi."

American QRF helicopters attacked Abdi Hassan's house on the morning of July 12 as Habr Gidr clan members discussed a peace initiative received from General Jonathan Howe, a retired American admiral now leading the UN mission in Mogadishu. Sixteen missiles fired into the house and killed many of the Habr Gidr but not Mad Abdi, who appeared briefly at about noon on September 29 but quickly disappeared into a crowd. Three days later, the SEALs geared up to hit Aidid at yet another house but never got the strike orders.

Wasdin installed some radio repeaters in the Lido district, an upscale beach district in Mogadishu, on the morning of October 3, not knowing that the longest day of his life was just ahead. When Wasdin returned to the operations center, Commander Olson ran up to Wasdin's M-998 Humvee troop carrier and ordered the mission personally. Wasdin, another SEAL called "Little Big Man," and three Rangers would serve as a blocking force for Delta operators assigned to grab some prisoners that day. "This shouldn't take long," Olson said. Four AH-6J Little Bird helicopters, each carrying four snipers and rockets underneath, would cover the front and rear doors of the target building while Delta operators fast-roped down to support the prisoner extraction. The Black Hawks, some eight birds in all, would then swoop in to insert more Delta team.

Wasdin had doubts about the mission, the sixth such operation carried out in broad daylight against experienced Aidid militiamen probably pumped up on khat. That afternoon, Wasdin rode just behind the leading three trucks. All told, nineteen aircraft, twelve vehicles, and 160 men were engaged, at least until the lead vehicle took a wrong turn.

The other drivers knew enough not to follow the leader, but no one expected what happened next. Just short of a traffic circle, AK-47 fire struck one of the SEALs, but they arrived at the Olympic Hotel, their mission destination otherwise unharmed, at 3:42 p.m. While Rangers fast-roped down and secured the four corners of the building, Wasdin settled into a sniper position, giving him a clear shot at the front door as an enemy sniper some five stories above the hotel began firing at the Americans, at least until Wasdin spotted and shot him.

Minutes later, two enemy militia on the fifth floor of an adjoining building began firing AK-47s at the Delta assault force outside the hotel. Wasdin shot them both before getting hit in the back of the knee himself. The beleaguered enemy militiamen began burning tires, a signal asking for militia reinforcements, as the Americans started returning to the convoy vehicles. One of the other SEALs arrived next to Wasdin just in time to kill a nearby militiaman and help get Wasdin to his feet. Back at the convoy, an RPG struck one of the five-ton trucks while several prisoners climbed into other vehicles, including Aidid's top political adviser Omar Salad, Abdi Yusef Herse, and Mohammed Assan Awale.

The mission shifted from prisoner snatch to a rescue when Velvet Elvis, a Black Hawk piloted by Chief Warrant Officer Cliff Wolcott, was struck by an RPG at 4:30 that afternoon. Despite his wound and before leaving the mission location, Wasdin hobbled out of the Humvee to retrieve a shell-shocked young Ranger lying in a defensive position in a nearby alley. Wasdin drove a Humvee back by a different route through smoke smelling of burning tires and trash and past dead people and a donkey on the ground. Every Humvee and truck in the convoy carried wounded men, "young kids in a horrific fight," taking fire.

Wasdin could go only as fast as the Humvee in front of him; he shot at militia ducking in and out of side streets while he waited, nailing a few along the wash. But now some of the militia began building roadblocks. Several women approached them and then ducked so that militiamen behind them could fire on the convoy. The second time that happened, Wasdin killed eight women and four armed militia shortly before learning that a second Black Hawk, this one piloted by Mike Durant, had crashed.

By now, Wasdin and the men in his Humvee had gone through 300 rounds of 5.56-mm CAR-15 ammunition. One SEAL using an antiquated but effective M-14 rifle was completely out of ammunition. Worse yet, due to misdirection, the convoy drove in a circle and now approached the Olympic Hotel, which they just left, as American helicopters fired guns and rockets until their ammunition was depleted, then buzzed the militia six times with skids close enough to the ground to take a few enemy out. Yet the militia kept coming until one of them practically blew Wasdin's already injured leg off before Wasdin shot him twice between the eyes.

When Wasdin's convoy finally arrived back at the operations center after two failed efforts to find the two downed Black Hawks, some fifty injured Americans lay on the runway tarmac waiting for triage treatment as blood flowed like water out a Humvee tailgate. Later, Wasdin learned that during the Battle of Mogadishu, enemy forces killed eighteen Americans and wounded some eighty-five during the capture of at least four members of Aidid's leadership cadre. This had been accomplished without the full deployment of M-2 Bradley infantry fighting vehicles, M-1 Abram tanks, or AC-130 Spectre gunships. The Americans rescued the survivors of the first Black Hawk helicopter shot down. Somalians captured Mike Durant—the sole survivor of the second Black Hawk. They released him eleven days later on October 14. Aidid survived another three years.

Sixteen years later, in the memoir on which this chapter is largely based, Wasdin reflected back on how lucky he had been. He had been aboard a Sea King helicopter that crashed near Bermuda in 1986. Seven years later at Mogadishu, three other men died when the Aidid militia shot down one of the QRF helicopters. Days earlier that September in 1993, he had been spared when the same militia attacked the safe house the SEALs called Pasha. And finally, Wasdin lost a leg but came out of Operation Gothic Serpent alive.

Today, SEAL Team Six is more valuable than ever despite sometimes bending Navy rules and even international law, operating in the shadows to get things done and save lives.

CHAPTER SEVEN

The Caves of Zhawar Kili

Captain Bob Harward lived in Afghanistan long before January 2002. His father served many years earlier in Tehran as the American naval attaché to the shah of Iran's government. Harward went to the Tehran American high school in Iran, learning Farsi and Pashto, an eastern Iranian language spoken as one of two official languages in Afghanistan, the other being Dari. Harward hitchhiked around Afghanistan the summer before he reported to the Naval Academy at Annapolis after a brief stint at the Naval Academy Preparatory School in Newport, Rhode Island, his family's hometown. He started his naval career on USS *Scott* but became a member of BUD/S Class 128.

September 11, 2001, found Harward commanding Naval Special Warfare Group One in Coronado. The early days of Group One were ably described by Dick Couch and William Doyle in their 2014 book *Navy SEALS: Their Untold Story.*

The 9/11 attack soon brought Harward an assignment like no other in SEAL history. He would be operating some 500 miles from seawater deep in Afghanistan. Planning soon began for an insert about 150 miles northeast of Kandahar, the second-largest city in Afghanistan. A SEAL platoon would lead a mission into an al-Qaeda care complex in the Zhawar Kili Valley of Khost province. This target had been on planning maps for at least three years and with good reason. The caves bordered Pakistan, making al-Qaeda deployment into either country easy.

Harward headquartered Task Force K-Bar, first called the Combined Joint Special Operations Task Force–South, in Kandahar, named for the K-Bar military-issue knife carried by SEALs and Marines. SEAL Teams Two, Three, and Eight, as well as operators from the 1st Battalion, 3rd Special Forces Group, complemented forces from Norway, Canada, New Zealand, Germany, Denmark, and Turkey. Although K-Bar included some CIA operatives, the command-and-control structure has been described as SEAL-centric.

The caves that were targeted had been recently discovered south of Tora Bora. Three years earlier, American bombers and cruise missiles pounded Taliban and al-Qaeda bases established there. The bombers returned in 2001 after an American geologist identified a rock formation in an Osama bin Laden video. When fresh January 2002 intelligence suggested that al-Qaeda forces were fleeing through the Zhawar Kili Valley into Pakistan, the prospect of bagging Osama bin Laden himself prompted Harward to call for SEAL Lieutenant Chris Cassidy. Harward told him that Cassidy's platoon would go in before dawn the next day.

Ironically enough, the Zhawar Valley complex was constructed largely during the Russian occupation of Afghanistan, when the American government financed and supported Afghan rebels. In those early post-9/11 days, Cassidy and other SEALs sometimes bent the rules or ignored the normal procedures to get special missions out the front door and completed.

Now the prospect of taking out or capturing al-Qaeda leadership figures made this mission a top priority. On the afternoon of January 6, missiles and smart bombs boomed into Zhawar Kili Valley. During the early hours of January 7, three helicopter pilots in a remote corner of Kandahar International Airport waited, their engines idling. Soon, a seventy-five-man assault group divided up and climbed into three Marine CH-53 Super Stallions designed for heavy lifts and well suited for high-altitude missions in Afghanistan.

"Let's kick some ass!" said Harward, and with that, they lifted off, gaining altitude within the airport boundaries to minimize the prospect of enemy fire as much as possible. The three birds met a KC-130 fuel tanker plane just south of the Hindu Kush (no easy feat) just before predator drones detected ground movements at the head of the valley, where the force planned to land.

The Navy dusted off Plan B, a landing in the middle of the valley, meaning more time on foot but less chance of landing in a hot zone. Fifteen seconds after approaching the new insert point, the team established a perimeter of sorts as the choppers flew away. The Marine component of the operation consisted of fifty men, including at least one from the Kuwait operation. This ecumenical operation team even included two FBI agents, an Army chemical biology specialist, and a Navy linguist. Everyone carried enough PowerBars and water to survive at least a day, maybe longer.

TV crime drama fans of that era might have mistaken them for a SWAT team, complete with body armor, ammunition, and, of course, weapons. The Marines would provide sniping, blocking force, and close-quarters support inside caves or buildings if it came to that. First, they made their way through terrain far from ideal, searching for Taliban, walking through unyielding brick-hard dirt, and looking up at canyons perfect for any snipers looking for ideal targets.

Their Marine partners moved out first, sizing up possible defensive positions along the way. They couldn't get to the high ground quickly enough, moving along under the command of Lieutenant Commander Lou Talageda, who split his troops into two formations, left front and right front, with the SEALs in a diamond formation behind them, moving to the northwest entrance. By dark, the SEALs inspected some seventy cave entrances that seemingly lined the valley. These were not mere holes carved by nature over the centuries. Instead, many were self-sustaining military complexes, often reinforced with steel I beams and bricks, some as long as three football fields placed end to end. Many brimmed with artillery, antiaircraft guns, and even tanks, not to mention row upon row of ammunition crates. And they had only twelve hours to destroy it all. Later reports described amenities, including classrooms, jail cells, virtual hotel suites, passports, and even freshly cleaned clothes, all purposed for terrorist training and export missions. The SEALs had to search it all with flashlights; the operation started almost thirty-six hours earlier. Yet when K-Bar called in for an extraction, Harward asked

SEAL Lieutenant Commander Todd Seniff to scout the immediate area for a place secure enough to stay overnight. The Marines remembered a small abandoned village where a decent defensive perimeter could be established and called it in to Harward.

There would be no fresh supplies. Their digs for the next night were nothing more than a collection of huts inhabited by goats, chickens, and two cows that the villagers left behind while trying to escape the bombs dropped and cruise missiles fired by the Americans the previous day. All seventy-four settled in for the night, some on guard duty, others doing perimeter patrols, while back in Kandahar, Harward read reports estimating the al-Qaeda materials stocked away in the caves.

Although the night passed quietly, during a patrol the next morning on a ridge west of Zhawar Kili, a SEAL squad and some Marines caught sight of thirty armed al-Qaeda below them in the valley. The Afghans quickly spotted the SEALs and began firing without effect; by the time they positioned themselves some 350 yards away from the SEALs, four 500-pound bombs began to land on Taliban heads, leaving not a trace, except some sandals and a few body parts.

Once digital images of the vast quantities of supplies and munitions hidden beneath Zhawar Kili began to arrive at headquarters in Kandahar via satellite, the dubious senior leadership began speculating on where it all came from, eventually concluding that the shipment route started over the border in Pakistan. Seven days later, the SEALs destroyed or collapsed every cave discovered during the operation. Most of them lost fifteen to twenty pounds working twenty hours a day before the Marine MH-60s made the last of six trips from Kandahar to extract them. Harward later described Zhawar Kili as a major turning point in the SEALs' history, showing that they could plan and execute a large-scale, complex mission within a very short time frame. Chris Cassidy, one of the leaders, became an astronaut and completed six space walks.

CHAPTER EIGHT

The Hero's Path

Scott "Chris" Kyle, the best-known SEAL sniper in American history, was not the first. Mike Boynton became one of the first Navy SEALs to operate as a sniper during the 1965 American incursion into the Dominican Republic. That operation offered Boynton his first opportunity to see what he could do with an AR-15, later known as the M-16. During the decades that followed, other Navy SEALs who chose to become snipers trained much the way Boynton had. Brandon Webb also followed that path.

Born in Canada nine years after Boynton's 1965 Santa Domingo experience, Webb grew up in an adventurous family. After his freshman year at Ventura High School, he sailed with his parents from California to Cabo San Lucas, Mexico, and points beyond in the South Pacific. He even learned celestial navigation before his father kicked him off the boat at Tahiti after an argument. Back in California, he took a sea-diving job at age sixteen. "You should check out the SEALs," one of the crew told him, explaining who they were and what they did. Within days, Webb decided that he would do exactly that, as he later told readers in his book *The Red Circle*, written with John David Mann and often relied on in this chapter. Three years later, in March 1993, now a graduate of Ventura High, Webb traveled to Florida for basic training, even though he lived just a few hours north of San Diego, the site of an identical Navy boot camp. Several weeks later, Webb watched a SEAL recruitment video and decided to sign up for that too someday. After search-and-rescue training, Webb joined Helicopter Anti-Submarine Squadron Six duty on the destroyer USS *Abraham Lincoln*.

Mid-June 1997 found Webb in BUD/S training at Coronado; three years later, he got an unusual invitation. The SEALs, then short on snipers, recruited Webb, who did well enough in training and practice to become one. He had never even thought about becoming a sniper, but without a moment's hesitation, he said yes, knowing that the toughest training in the SEALs might consume his next three months. Physically less challenging than BUD/S or SEAL tactical training, sniper school develops the mental capacity to spend days enduring hardship.

The first phase of the training focused on weapons, ballistics, and marksmanship, splitting Webb and twenty-five other SEALs into pairs that rotated between shooting and spotting. The second training phase taught stalking, stealth, and concealment. Only twelve graduated. They trained on M-14s, Remington 308 bolt-action guns, and two other scoped weapons. That training was not wasted on Webb, who returned to SEAL Team Three for an October 12, 2000, deployment on USS *Duluth* to the Mideast. That very morning, while the destroyer USS *Cole* refueled in the Gulf of Aden, two laughing men in a speedboat carrying explosives struck *Cole* and killed seventeen sailors, injuring thirty-nine others. Eight hours later, Webb and his SEAL Team Three jumped into boats on the Yemini coast, speeding toward *Cole* to establish a 500-meter parameter. Webb and another sniper set up a post on the ship's bridge, armed with rifles and rockets. They rotated duty with another team every twelve hours as other sailors repaired the forty- by forty-foot hole in the port side of the hull at an eventual cost of about $250 million.

A few Yemeni boats tested the perimeter briefly, but no one attacked *Cole* again that night. Webb soon discovered that at the time of the attack, no perimeter protected the ship, nor were there any armed men on the *Cole*'s deck at the time of the attack. Webb also learned that a similar attempted attack planned at the same port twelve months earlier had failed. USS *Sullivans*, a guided-missile destroyer named for four brothers who died courageously during World War II, survived only because the speedboat, overloaded with explosives, foundered and sank.

Back at home in California with his wife, Brandon watched the second plane hit the South Tower of the World Trade Center on September 11. Several days later, his SEAL Team Three platoon deployed to Afghanistan. Twenty hours after arriving there, planners briefed them in Camp Dora, Kuwait, about their first mission in the Persian Gulf. They would be intercepting Iraqi oil smugglers; often, the smugglers bolted or even welded car doors shut to keep Americans from taking control. Assigned local interpreters called the SEALs and the Rangers on this mission "the White Devils." The entire mixed-force team wore "FDNY" patches on their uniforms.

White Devils they might be, but the SEALs dressed in black from head to foot, including masks. Their operations deployed at sunset in small Mark V boats carrying sixteen SEALs into the international shipping lanes, waiting for targets to arrive. The snipers conducted a separate supporting mission while sitting at open cargo doors of Sea Hawk helicopters nearby, using forward-looking infrared systems to pass along the positions of targets. They helped take down six smuggling vessels within a few weeks before the *Alpha-117* mission arrived.

The target: an al-Qaeda vessel smuggling explosives that blew up U.S. embassies in Tanzania and Nairobi in 1998, killing more than 200 people. And now, according to National Security Agency intelligence, the tanker *Alpha-117* might be departing Iraq with yet another large cache of explosives. There was no confusion about the orders. If *Alpha-117* appeared in their lane, the SEALs must take it down.

The next night, while pulling Sea Hawk duty, Webb looked down at the pale green screen of the forward-looking infrared and read the numbers on a vessel below them: *Alpha-117*. He radioed the platoon commander, who in turn contacted a destroyer miles away. Soon, future NASA astronaut Chris Cassidy radioed Webb to initiate the mission in spite of some significant danger. In these same waters, Webb had participated earlier in a training exercise in which a chopper dipped into the drink, averting a crash only by shooting straight up into the air just in time. Webb, now in charge of surveillance, laid out the possible course of action for Cassidy. Estimating the *Alpha-117*'s speed at about eighteen knots (twenty miles per hour), Webb recommended that the attacking SEAL boats "double-hook" the enemy vessel fore and aft. Webb later described the mission as pulling a Hummer next to a bus going sixty miles per hour while six SEALs boarded the bus in full gear. Webb could have also mentioned that the Sea Hawk helicopter hovered in the darkness about fifteen feet above.

The empty *Alpha-117* deck welcomed the SEAL assault teams fore and aft now moving toward the bridge and aft steering below. Webb watched transfixed as explosives and gunfire lit up the wheelhouse, but the pilot, who heard but could not see this, thought the fire was directed at the Sea Hawk and pulled up, nearly throwing Webb out the open cargo door into the water or, worse yet, onto the open *Alpha-117* deck.

Webb watched SEAL Team Three take control of the ship and then strip the captain of his hat, his M-4, and even his cigar. The SEALs took a total of thirty prisoners that night, along with fake passports, dozens of weapons, and more than $100,000.

When Operation Enduring Freedom began on October 7, Webb and his platoon deployed to Oman; soon, they departed for Kandahar Airport, base of operations for Task Force K-Bar.

K-Bar included Special Forces from eight different countries. The rules of engagement for this operation seemed a bit unusual. Any local male fifteen years or older within 500 feet of any U.S. vessel should be considered a potential target. This contrasted sharply with the restrictions normally imposed on SEAL operations. Webb and the other SEALs soon learned that local tribal leaders would sometimes settle decades-old scores by falsely identifying rival tribal leaders as al-Qaeda or Taliban fighters.

His first action on the ground came in mid-December at Kandahar Airport, down-ramping from the C-130 through blood pools and broken glass as helicopters bringing in troops and equipment dodged trucks and Jeeps hurried around the runway. The Soviets had abandoned this land mine–infested airfield more than a decade earlier. The SEALs and Army Special Forces units set up a shantytown complete with makeshift showers, fire pits, and lounges while they waited for the first mission. Rotting MIGs, Soviet tanks, and AK-47s surrounded them. Just before the SEALs arrived, Americans installed guard towers and barbed wire. The airport served as a staging area for prisoners being sent to Guantanamo Bay, Cuba.

Webb's SEAL platoon spent Christmas evening 2001 on convoy patrol through high desert, lugging rocket launchers and Mark 41 automatic grenade guns and communication equipment linking them to the operations center via satellite; two Air Force Combat Control Team pathfinders, ready to bring in air support if needed, accompanied them. Early the next morning, they stopped at a river to survey a small grove of trees standing among sand dunes on the opposite bank. Webb considered it a probable Taliban or al-Qaeda campsite, as confirmed later by campfires. A few days later, they nearly died at a place call Tarnak Farm near Kandahar Airport, which served as a base of operations for Osama bin Laden in the three years prior to 9/11. Al-Qaeda equipped the place with monkey bars and even an obstacle course, but the SEALs and other American forces used it to test weapons and destroy enemy ordnance.

Eight of them loaded up enemy ordnance for a trip to Tarnak Farm a few days before New Year's Day. When they parked, Webb noticed something unusual beneath one of the Humvee rear tires. The detonating cord led to an antitank mine that might have killed them all if correctly assembled. Webb realized that just a few days before, an Explosive Ordnance Disposal team cleared this area. Al-Qaeda was back in the area, but Webb's SEAL Team Three platoon now pushed toward the caves of Zhawar Kili, near Khost, some 2,734 miles northeast of Kandahar. Webb later described the caves as a base camp comprised of three large tunnels, containing arms depots, communications equipment, hotel-like rooms, medical facilities, and even a mosque.

Soviet missions to storm the caves were only marginally more successful than those conducted by their Afghan puppet government. The Russians forced the mujahideen to flee before planting land mines to discourage a rebel return. Now, in early January 2002, two months after air strikes, the Americans launched a new effort.

Originally, the reconnaissance mission to explore the caves and bring back refined air strike coordinates was assigned to a Green Beret team that was no longer available, having been deployed on a direct-action mission against a Taliban-controlled compound.

Twenty Marines, two Air Force combat controllers, an Explosive Ordnance Disposal team duo, two FBI agents for forensics and DNA work-ups, and an Army Chemical Reconnaissance Detachment expert on chemical weapons supplemented Webb's SEAL Team Three platoon of sixteen. The plan called for a U.S. Marine perimeter, an assessment to verify the damage done in an October 7 bomb run, and ten-hour cave reconnaissance, all within twelve hours door-to-door. A SEAL lieutenant commander who was put in charge of the mission at the last minute ordered everyone to fully suit up in Kevlar body armor, even though they would be dropped into a breath-consuming 12,000-foot-altitude battle space carrying extra equipment, weapons, and munitions.

The planned one-hour insertion began a 1:00 a.m. on Sunday, July 6, but put them at the target at about 4:00 a.m. Webb quietly pulled the armor plates out of his Kevlar suit, unlike teammates who wore themselves out climbing up the mountain trails toward the caves.

Their door crasher ("breacher") carried a huge metal tool called a hooligan and a heavy load of explosives. The team also carried cameras to record everything they did. Just before reaching the caves, the lieutenant commander ordered everyone to hide their armor. They reached the flat caves at dawn around 6:30 a.m. This lower cave complex had been saturated by air strikes the prior evening, but nothing but scattered body parts remained.

The caves above them on a ridge presented more challenges, often being steel reinforced and lined with bricks, possibly even installed by the Russians, according to Webb. The SEALs cleared cave after cave, moving serially through the complex, some of which connected ammunition bunkers, living quarters, and even classrooms, now all in empty darkness, brightened only by small lights on their weapons and even smaller flashlights.

The SEALs worked in groups of four, finding ordnance, fuel, Soviet combat vehicles, and even tanks. More surprising, they found highly sensitive Harris-117 radios, which the CIA had encrypted for Afghan mujahideen resisting the ten-year Soviet invasion that began in 1979. One recruiting poster featured bin Laden superimposed in front of two planes crashing into the World Trade Center's twin towers. After four hours clearing all the upper-altitude caves, SEAL Team Three and the other operations began planting demolition. Hour 7 of the planned ten-hour operation came and went.

Soon, headquarters canceled their extraction. Captain Bob Harward, the SEAL Team Three commanding officer in charge of the caves operation, wanted some grave sites that had been discovered during the operation searched for any evidence that the team killed higher-level al-Qaeda leaders. They would be staying at least another day or so even though they carried no overnight gear and only one meal. Webb was better equipped than many of the others, sporting $300 Italian leather mountain boots, but where could they spend the night? After a heated discussion, team leader Lieutenant Cassidy sent several men to occupy a village they had passed through on their way up the mountain.

Webb and four others climbed an hour farther up the mountain to get there, but the abandoned huts offered perfect visibility and a highly defensible position, not to mention wool blankets, firewood, and fireplaces to keep the chill out.

The new mission seemed like a day at the beach—at least until Webb and four others encountered twenty enemy fighters pouring out of a cave that the SEALs had not cleared. Webb quickly went into sniper mode, dropping three out of twenty, while the Americans waited for a B-52 to drop a bomb Webb had requested by radio. Just before the bomb killed the fighters, Webb heard a baby cry—for the last time. The SEALs returned to Kandahar with nine new prisoners despite orders from a Marine general nicknamed "Mad Dog" not to bring back any. General Mattis later became U.S. secretary of defense in the Trump administration.

Several days into the extended reconnaissance mission, Webb realized that he had narrowly missed death twice. On the way up to the village, they passed a heavily armed Taliban campsite the Taliban later abandoned, leaving behind documents, hand grenades, AK-47s, and even a warm teapot. The day before, on January 9, four Taliban no doubt spotted Webb and four other SEALs from a hiding spot Webb discovered the next day but, for reasons unknown, ran for the Pakistani border rather than opening fire.

After days of routine reconnaissance, Webb went into sniper mode on Friday, January 11, aiming a .300 Win Mag sniper rifle at men in a village from an overwatch position as several other SEALs approached. One of the targets lugged a gun. Webb, about 600 yards away, put the man in his sight and waited for the slightest sign that the villager intended to open fire. That twitch, that gesture, that motion, never came. And so the villager lived at least another day.

On day 7 of the ten-hour operation, Saturday, January 12, Webb proposed that he and another SEAL named Osman scout a suspected Taliban checkpoint that Webb had spotted earlier. Wearing Afghan robes, Webb and Osman also sported a special reflective infrared tape by which American "eyes in the sky" could distinguish the SEALs from the Taliban targets they might be bombing.

Soon, they watched a middle-aged Taliban fighter limping away from the suspected checkpoint. Webb later recalled scouting about five other small Taliban camps that day before returning to the SEAL camp at midnight. During the wee hours of Sunday, January 13, Webb and Osman visually verified all six sites they had scouted earlier, now marked by the light of cook stoves and campfires. And one by one, F-18 Hornet Jets destroyed each site. The SEAL Team Three platoon and the other Americans left on January 14, concluding a mission that uncovered almost a million pounds of material in seventy caves and tunnels no longer available to the Taliban.

Back in Kandahar, Osman, Webb, and the other SEALs soon began working with a German Special Operations team on a new high-value-target mission. Prata Ghar, a village a few miles north of Zhawar Kili, was the site of yet another cave complex; the village center was a four-story building amidst several smaller ones. The plan assigned the central building to the Germans. The SEAL Team Three platoon would take care of the rest during the wee hours of January 24. The whole operation relied on a lone photograph.

A total of a dozen buildings were cleared. The SEALs proceeded quickly, room by room, waking up sleeping villagers, many of them terrified women and children. They learned that the high-value targets the SEALs had sought departed a day earlier, leaving a large cache of weapons behind. Minutes later, while Webb and several others retrieved gear from a nearby ravine, some fifty locals, most carrying weapons, gathered and began glaring as an elder screamed in Pashtu. Surrounded by twenty times their number, the special operators backed them off only by firing into the ground just in front of the Afghans in the first row.

The next day, the snow gear they needed for the mission that they had just completed arrived in Kandahar, none of it the size ordered. Several days later, the combined German-American Special Operations Team climbed into several Sikorsky H-53 helicopters for a ride to Ahmed Kheyl, yet another cave complex north of Zhawar Kili. A blond, green-eyed local Afghan government commander, possibly descended from Europeans who invaded that region with Alexander the Great in 330 BCE, met them. They trudged 3,500 feet up the mountain in several feet of snow, finding the caves abandoned as expected. For Webb, the war in Afghanistan now ended, but in the film *American Sniper*, Wayne Kenneth Kyle, father of Scott "Chris" Kyle, described the road that Chris and many SEALs traveled:

> *If you have no capacity for violence, then you are a healthy productive citizen: a sheep. If you have a capacity for violence and no empathy for your fellow citizens, then you have defined an aggressive sociopath—a wolf. But what if you have a capacity for violence and a deep love for your fellow citizens? Then you are a warrior, someone who is walking the hero's path.*

CHAPTER NINE

The Terminals

Saddam Hussein knew the Americans were coming. He had ordered Iraqi Scud bombardments of Kuwait two days before, on March 21, 2003, the date when the United States invaded his country. The main worry about the Scuds: the possibility of their carrying chemical weapons that Saddam had used on his own people years earlier. Yet the Navy SEALs waiting at Ali al-Salim Air Base in Kuwait were eager to start the mission and capture critical oil facilities in Iraq. Years later, Bob Harward, who became a vice admiral in 2011, described this mission as the largest combat operation in U.S. Navy SEAL history, comparable to the larger amphibious operations in the Pacific during World War II.

Soon after the Scuds arrived, eight SEALs boarded a helicopter with eight British Royal Marines, an aircraft combat controller, and a Navy Explosive Ordnance Disposal man. Three weeks earlier, SEALs on the Air Force MH-53 Pave Low helicopter in Okinawa trained with Japanese forces while many others prepared for action. Now the SEALs and their teammates learned the gravity and complexities of their mission.

Four different teams would be attacking two terminals. Each terminal consisted of a petroleum pumping lock (essentially a huge spigot) onshore and a loading platform about twelve miles out in the Persian Gulf connected by a pipeline. The Al Basrah Oil Terminal was built in 1974 to service four crude oil carriers at once. MABOT (Mina al-Bakr Oil Terminal) floated some thirty-one miles southeast of the Al-Faw peninsula on the Persian Gulf. The Americans also targeted a land terminal, called KAAOT (an abbreviation of Khor al-Amaya), seven miles away, as described in *Down Range*, written by Dick Couch and largely relied on in this chapter. Two SEAL teams would seize the MABOT pumping station onshore, the MABOT platform offshore, and two similar KAAOT facilities. The SEALs were tasked to neutralize Iraqi forces guarding the Iraqi oil export facilities so that Saddam could not have them destroyed.

Lieutenant (junior grade) Craig Thomas, who led the squad a few minutes after midnight that March 21, had graduated from the Naval Academy four years earlier and joined BUD/S Class 228. Everyone on the Thomas chopper carried demolition supplies, rockets, and grenades. Their Kevlar vests and helmets weighed thirty pounds. Everyone held on to the helicopter bench seats to avoid falling over. The Thomas chopper hovered above a landing area covered by barbed wire, probably just laid out by the defending Iraqis. Six Royal Marines jumped into the barbed wire, making themselves into walking mats for the rest of the men deploying, even as enemy rounds began popping over their heads. Others quickly established a perimeter within which the SEALs began preparing for the assault; still other Royal Marines conducted a similar operation at the nearby KAAOT pumping station on land. Each of the two oil platform complexes that were rigged to explode could load as much as 1.6 million barrels of oil onto tankers in a single day. Experts estimated that in a worst-case scenario, an oil spill twelve times worse than the March 1989 *Exxon Valdez* spill might result, stymieing the new democratic Iraqi government the Americans hoped for.

The March 21 operation followed reconnaissance two days earlier. Mark VIII SDVs surfaced near the MABOT and KAAOT platform complexes strung out over two miles so that SEAL SDV reconnaissance crews could listen in on the defense teams after tying their boats to the platform legs. They even took photographs. Practically speaking, the MABOT platform in the Persian Gulf consisted of four structures connected by latticework. The first structure was a helicopter platform, and the second, some 300 meters farther out in the ocean, was a loading station stretching the length of a football field and capable of fueling two supertankers at once. The third structure was identical to the second. All three structures were served by a crew living on the four-story fourth structure farthest out to sea. The reconnaissance mission to the MABOT platform found no explosives, but the SEALs couldn't rule out the possibility that detonation devices were embedded in the structures themselves.

Two hours before the Thomas team started their midnight run to the onshore MABOT pumping station on March 20, Lieutenant Chuck Forbes and his team drifted 300 yards away from the MABOT oil platform twelve miles out in the Persian Gulf—the key installation. Forbes was a Mustang: an enlisted man eventually commissioned as an officer. After graduating from SEALs training in 1984, he became one of the few men then serving as a male nurse but began training to become a SEAL platoon commander in 1994. The MABOT oil platform operation offered Forbes the opportunity to make up for lost time. A total of 250 men from the U.S. Marines, the British Royal Marines, the Polish Special Forces, and the U.S. Navy SEALs would be occupying the MABOT and KAAOT facilities on land and sea. In theory, the attacks would be simultaneous.

— ◆ —

Forbes and forty-eight other SEALs, just outside the glare projected from the highly illuminated MABOT platform, crouched in heavily laden boats that could be spotted any minute by the Iraqis. While drifting right into the bright lights of a city at sea, Forbes wondered why he hadn't received the attack order yet. Intelligence reports said that Republican Guards aboard the platforms carried heavy weapons and RPGs that might blow the SEALs out of the water if anybody detected them. Soon after Forbes convinced Captain Harward to green-light the attack, six boats roared toward the access ladder, and SEALs and others climbed upward and spread out across the platform. After everyone on board surrendered, the SEALs discovered AK-47s, explosives, and even heat-seeking aircraft missiles. Lieutenant Thomas and the others accomplished their MADOT and KAAOT missions, even as yet another team comprised of SEALs and Polish Special Forces occupied the Mukkarin hydroelectric project northeast of Baghdad. Two days later, a soldier named Jessica Lynch experienced something far different.

CHAPTER TEN

Wrong Turn

SHE WOULD BE TWENTY YEARS OLD IN A MONTH, BUT THIS WAS THE last thing on her mind as Jessica pushed the five-ton diesel truck across barren ground on the road to Baghdad. The 507th Maintenance Company had been deployed from Kuwait, trailing behind most of a massive convoy carrying food, fuel, and even toilet paper for the GIs carrying out Operation Iraqi Freedom on Sunday, March 23, 2003. The RPGs showering Jessica's segment of the convoy seemed to come out of nowhere, as did AK-47 fire from Iraqis on nearby roofs when the convoy missed a turn on the road to Baghdad. Her best friend, Lori Ann Piestewa, a Hopi Indian from Tuba City, Arizona, soon spotted Jessica and stopped to pick her up. But then, a grinding noise beneath her Humvee rose from a rumble to a screech just before grinding to a halt. "Get in!" Lori yelled. Jessica was in downtown Nasiriyah, a town of half a million on the north bank of the Euphrates River, full of Saddam supporters.

The day began at Camp Virginia in central Kuwait. Their mission once they reached their destination: maintenance support of Patriot missiles controlled by the 2nd Battalion, 7th Air Defense Artillery. The plan called for a quick rush to Baghdad, 191 miles northwest of Nasiriyah, but now the convoy stalled and stopped. Jessica and Lori soon joined other soldiers who piled out of their vehicles to surround and guard a truck that ran out of gas. The women stood back-to-back, shoulder-to-shoulder, sinking in red clay and sand, outnumbered at least five to one.

A few minutes later, Lori began pushing the Humvee forward again as Jessica looked back at everyone left behind. Many Americans were dead or soon would be. Within minutes, hostiles captured Jessica, her friend Lori, and four others. Jessica never saw Lori again. Some six days later, an Iraqi attorney, thirty-two-year-old Mohammed Odeh al Rehaief, approached some Americans at a U.S. Marine checkpoint six miles outside of town. He reported that an American woman was being held at a hospital in Nasiriyah. Mohammed returned later with maps, hospital sketches, and hospital shift-change information.

Task Force 20 carried out the Nasiriyah rescue mission in joint operations from Talil Air Base about twelve miles from where Lynch pondered her fate. The task force learned that Fedayeen Saddam, irregular forces who reported directly to Saddam Hussein, occupied the hospital basement. Created eight years earlier as a response to Operation Iraqi Freedom, the Fedayeen replaced the Iraqi Republican Forces, which had quickly evaporated. Task force planners calculated that some 488 SEAL Team Six, Rangers, Marines, and Delta and Army personnel would participate. The SEAL Gold Team would lead the mission, relying solely on a brief video of the route from the hospital entrance to Lynch's hospital room.

The operation began with an April 1 diversionary attack on the south bank of the Euphrates shortly after midnight, just as the Marines cut off all power in Nasiriyah. The hospital gave the Gold Team a perfect target by turning on its generators.

Soon, two MH-6 Little Bird helicopters, each carrying three Gold Team SEALs, landed in front of the main door as a Black Hawk dropped Gold Team snipers on the roof of Saddam General Hospital, where surgeons stabilized her shattered leg on March 23 by inserting a steel rod. Three doctors and two nurses bravely told Iraqi soldiers that she could not be moved.

And now, in the early morning gloom of April 1, Jessica awoke in her hospital room listening to noises she did not understand. The noises became louder. She heard someone come into the room but couldn't see who was there. "Jessica!" said a voice that sounded American as she related later in *I Am a Soldier Too*, a book written with Rick Bragg that very year. An American walked in the light and took off his combat helmet.

The SEAL Gold Team had arrived.

CHAPTER ELEVEN

A Good Deed Punished

MARCUS (MARK) LUTTRELL HAD TRAINED TO SAVE LIFE AND TO TAKE it as platoon medic and sniper for SEAL SDV Team 1, Alfa (not Alpha) Platoon. Now he rode in an unarmored vehicle across Manama, the capital of Bahrain, to an American air base on Muharraq Island, just outside of town. In March 2005, Luttrell and five others loaded their machine guns, pistols, ammunition belts, and knives into a noisy C-130 Hercules. Some of the guys struck up net hammocks for the ride to come. They detoured around Iran, crossing the United Arab Emirates instead, toward Iraq. Special Forces Command (SPECWARCOM) recently assigned them this mission without briefing them on the details. The five heavily bearded men flying into danger included Matthew Gene (Axe) Axelson, a sergeant from California. Lieutenant Michael Patrick Murphy graduated from Pennsylvania State University but joined the Navy instead of going to one of the law schools that had accepted him. Daniel Richard (Danny) Healy, the senior chief and the father of seven children, researched and planned many of their missions. Shane Patton, a petty officer, served as Mark's communication specialist; Danny liked weird stuff, like leopard-skin coats. James Suru grew up in South Florida and chose to join the SEALs instead of becoming a veterinarian. They soared over the Gulf of Oman three hours after boarding the C-130, heading due south of the Iranian border. Luttrell was a native of East Texas. His twin brother was also a Navy SEAL. Their father, an all-American swimmer in high school, taught the twins scuba diving and one enduring principle: nothing happens unless you make it happen.

The Taliban-affiliated fighters ("Taliban") they soon might be facing also lived by that same principle but with different objectives. The Taliban and their affiliates wanted to run Afghanistan again. The previous month, in February 2005, the Taliban had launched a successful series of bombings and assassinations targeting local politicos and mullahs. The term "Taliban" means "students," but their interest gravitated toward weapons and executions more than books. Now, the Taliban, their allies, and their affiliates became increasingly visible in southern and eastern Afghanistan, attacking foreign construction workers and NGO workers.

The C-130 lumbered at daylight into Bagram Air Base, a few miles outside of the town destroyed by Cyrus the Great around 550 BCE and rebuilt by Alexander the Great 221 years later. Mark carried a portable DVD player and his favorite movie, *The Count of Monte Cristo*. During the SEAL Team Ten operational read-in on current operations, the briefers confirmed that the Taliban on the craggy cliffs above them looked for any chance to kill Americans wherever and whenever possible. That very day, Luttrell and the other newbies joined a helicopter mission patrolling nearby valleys as part of a twenty-man mission. They jumped out about a mile from the Pakistani border to patrol a high pass clearly visible to any Taliban in the valley below. Within minutes, three Afghans some seventy yards beneath them opened fire with AK-47s, followed by RPGs. Mark waited for them to break cover, and when they did, the team killed all three. Soon, Luttrell and the other SEALs joined forty-four other men on a routine mountain patrol before being ordered to join Foxtrot Platoon. Their first Foxtrot mission: find and capture a Taliban explosives expert who recently ambushed two Marine convoys. Intelligence indicated that the target slept in one of two Afghan villages on a mountain, one above the other. Foxtrot Platoon raided the upper village at sunrise but didn't find the Taliban munitions man they wanted. SEAL Team Ten found him trying to hide among mountain-hardened goat herds in the lower village. He didn't even have a beard.

In later weeks, they launched operations whenever a full moon enabled nighttime operations. Lieutenant Commander Eric Kristensen called this ongoing operation Lone Star to kid East Texas native Luttrell, on whose memoir, descriptions of names and places, and versions of events this chapter is largely although not exclusively based. After some time in country, Luttrell could spot the Taliban hit men, like the explosions expert they called "Abdul, the Bombmaker." The sullen and bearded Taliban seldom could be confused with men who worked outdoors regularly. Some of the American-hating Taliban even held degrees conferred in the United States. Night patrols around villages could be dangerous since nearly invisible communal bathroom pits loomed everywhere. Even though he used night-vision goggles, Luttrell stumbled into two such pits. More often than not, in Luttrell's experience, Americans patrolling near Pakistan came under fire from across the border.

Dan Healy and the other SEAL team leaders sifted intelligence to identify the most credible Taliban targets. Starting with lists, Healy scrutinized photographs, maps, charts, and venues, developing a short list of Taliban bosses for the June 2005 Taliban hunting season. One likely target: Ahmad Shah, code-named "Ben Sharmak," a forty-something local commander affiliated loosely with the Taliban. Ben spoke five languages. Operation Red Wings, named for the Detroit hockey team, began searching for Shah. Four Alfa Platoon men carried out the reconnaissance mission, hoping to "nail down" his location if possible before calling in reinforcements to take out Sharmak's Taliban troops.

Several false starts by intelligence frustrated Luttrell and the others beyond words. At least the team, consisting of Luttrell, Murphy Axelson, and newcomer Danny Dietz, was finalized. After one more false start, sources spotted Sharmak on Monday, June 25. "This is it, we're going," they were told. Luttrell and the others mounted up for a mission to the Hindu Kush, which reportedly means "Hindu killer," a reference to slaves from the Indian continent who died crossing Afghan mountains while trudging toward central Asia. The team surveyed a village of about thirty houses, equipped for the mission with solid Global Positioning System data, but logistical challenges were everywhere. Trees would have to be knocked down for a possible helicopter extraction; worse yet, the barren, vegetation-free mountaintop offered no place to hide from Shah's militia, whose numbers reportedly consisted of between eighty and 200 fighters. Photographs of the steep, bare ground made at least one of Luttrell's team members nervous.

———

That evening, they climbed into a Chinook 47 to be dropped at the target destination forty-five minutes away; three "false start" inserts at places near (but not near enough to) the planned landing zone gave Taliban fighters a clear warning that the Americans were coming. On the fourth try, the team roped down to the landing zone in the moonless darkness, wondering how many Taliban gunmen watched from hidey-holes around them. The chopper clattered away, leaving them a rope that might later betray their presence to the Taliban if not hidden quickly. Fifteen minutes later, Luttrell saw another problem.

This wasn't the landing zone, either. The helicopter simply dropped the landing rope instead of pulling it up; the SEALs were forced to cover it with dirt before beginning the four-mile trip up the mountain, occasionally falling a few feet back downward. They moved slowly, even though three of the four were highly experienced mountain climbers.

They finally reached a cliff face and a foot path. A new problem confronted the SEALs a few minutes later as they stared at a huge tall-grass prairie; the moonlit clouds above made the place tranquil—almost. Axelson quietly scouted for a path but couldn't find one, fearing the whole time that Taliban might be hiding there in ambush. Finally, just as the moon disappeared, one of them found a path around and down the backside of the mountain to the village and their target, Ahmad Shah.

During a heavy rain that now started, Luttrell and his team nearly stumbled into an Afghan farmhouse but saw it in time to low-crawl in the mud around it. Their night optic devices guided the way around trouble spots; this gave them an advantage against those who might have spotted them but for the rain, at least until the moon came out again, just as they walked into a clearing. Now the SEALs, silhouetted against a treeless mountainside above a Taliban-occupied village in stark moonlight, faced even greater danger. Somehow undetected, they edged along the path up and down the backside of the hill step-by-step, inching slowly through rough, extremely steep terrain, around cliffs, far away from their preplanned position.

They zigged and zagged up and down the mountainside, avoiding cliffs while trying to find the least rocky, safest path to lug heavy loads to "waypoint 3" on the brow of a steep summit. The four-mile hike in the dark took about seven hours, exhausting all of them. While the others shivered in wet clothing, Dietz radioed in their position, but the mission command controller decided that due to recent logging in the area, this preplanned position was far too exposed. They moved to another location a mile and a half away in trees above the targeted village. When fog blocked their view a few minutes later, they moved yet again to a place a third of a mile away back up the mountain on a ridge. Although the move took an entire hour, the new venue offered perfect scope viewing; that said, the barren, stony ground offered no camouflage, and the only escape route wound back down the way they came. The SEALs spread out across the position.

Luttrell set up his sniping position just beneath a felled log with Murphy about fifty yards away on a higher position. Axelson and Dietz were to Luttrell's left behind trees as they looked down at the village at high noon in the Hindu Kush. The wisecracks just started when Luttrell heard the distant but unmistakable sound of footsteps just above him, only to turn and see a turbaned Afghan carrying an ax. A fourteen-year-old boy, two men, and a herd of goats quickly surrounded the SEALs. Now what? They were soft compromised, a hard compromise being a direct, armed attack.

—◆—

"No Taliban! No Taliban," one of the obviously hostile captives said as both men glared at Luttrell and Murphy. The kid scowled at a PowerBar that Luttrell gave him. Lieutenant Murphy polled his crew while trying to decide what to do. These were either Taliban or unarmed civilians with an attitude. Axelson and Luttrell initially favored killing them, Dietz expressed no opinion one way or another, but in the end Murphy decided to let them go in accordance with the Geneva Convention. Luttrell, thinking that there might be as many as 200 men in the village below, asked Murphy to call in for some advice, but no one answered their radio call.

Without a word, the captives began climbing back up the steep gradient. Luttrell regretted how he voted even as he watched a mangy brown dog fall in line behind the teenager. Ahmad Shah, their target, was nowhere to be seen. "Move in five," Murphy told them, and so they did, more or less following the goat herds the SEALs just released. They called the base again but heard only silence. Now they became fugitives on the run. The best place to hide was forty yards or so below the mountain summit on a ridge that offered a few trees for concealment—or so they thought. There wasn't as much concealment in the afternoon daylight as they had hoped for, but it was all they had, and from the top of the mountain escarpment, they would be invisible—almost.

A brief silence followed but didn't last. Soon, Murphy hissed to Luttrell and then pointed his rifle at the ridge above them, where, according to Luttrell's recollections, as many as 100 Taliban warriors pointed AK-47s down the hill toward them. Some also carried RPGs. The hard-compromised SEALs now faced significant danger. As the Taliban began flanking them, Luttrell could see the trap. Luttrell killed the first Taliban that day with a head shot, while AK-47 fire poured down on the SEALs from everywhere above, left and right. The Taliban appeared on the ridge again and again, replacing others whom the SEALs shot down, before Murphy barked an order.

"Fall back," he yelled, and so they did, starting down the mountain. Murphy and Luttrell rolled and tumbled, Murphy sometimes below Luttrell and other times behind him. And now the two of them crashed through a copse of trees that stripped Murphy of their lifeline: the radio. A fall down a small cliff was next before Murphy and Luttrell came to a halt about 300 yards from where they started. When Luttrell stood up, the Taliban began showering them with RPGs and rifle fire from their flanks. Most missed by feet if not yards, but Murphy was shot in the stomach. They found two crossed logs to hide behind while shooting everyone coming down the mountain. These Taliban made terrible marksmen but excelled at logistics, outflanking Murphy and Luttrell, surrounding them as they kept up a constant volley of fire.

Within minutes, Luttrell recalled later, Axelson and Dietz rolled down and joined him in the fight.

The extra firepower emboldened the four SEALs to assault the Taliban left flank in an escape attempt, but after a brief firefight, the turbaned ones forced them back to the crossed logs. Luttrell said later that with a dozen SEALs instead of four, they could have held out, but now they had to abandon the crossed logs and jump off another cliff. After coming to a stop and untangling themselves, the quartet spread out to maximize their firing position just before Healy, who had already lost his right thumb, was shot in the back. Taliban reinforcements fighting from high ground poured in more fire, hitting Dietz a third time, but Dietz kept firing. The only SEAL option left was getting down to the village for a last stand in one of the houses. They cliff-jumped again while Dietz provided covering fire.

Axelson, the thinnest of the four, crawled under a hollow log toward the next cliff down on the mountain beneath them. Luttrell, more stout than Axelson, tried to do the same thing, even as RPGs began landing around him, one close enough to blow him over the cliff, breaking his nose. The worst was yet to come. While dragging Dietz out of the direct line of fire, Luttrell confronted a Taliban warrior smiling over his AK-47, but Axelson took him out with two shots between the eyes. Within seconds, Luttrell saw Dietz die but had to leave him behind. Axelson, shot in the chest minutes earlier, provided cover as Luttrell skidded down the hill toward a stream. And then he told both Axelson and Murphy that Danny was dead.

SEALs never leave anyone behind if there is any choice. Luttrell blurted out the obvious truth: either they must get off this mountain and into the village, or they might be dead too. Now as many as sixty Taliban surrounded them, firing down from the hill as well as from above and tossing grenades ever closer.

Luttrell and the other two survivors crouched behind rocks some two miles above the village and 1,000 yards from flat ground. Once again, they moved back up into the canyon to escape gunfire. That's when

Lieutenant Murphy sacrificed his life to get help for the other two. He walked into a clearing to get cell phone reception, reported their position to the operations center, and killed several of the Taliban. "Roger that, sir, thank you," Murphy said after being shot in the back. He fought on even though blood spurted from his chest. Axelson, mortally wounded by then, the right side of his head practically gone, lurched toward some rocks, no longer carrying his rifle. Murphy spent his last few minutes alive screaming for help that Luttrell couldn't give him without getting killed himself. When Murphy died, Luttrell moved back downhill under fire to the place where Axelson was hiding, resolved to die there with him, firing at any Taliban he could spot along the way. "You stay alive, Marcus," Axelson said, "and tell Cindy I love her." Then he too was gone, at age twenty-nine, just as a Russian grenade landed nearby, knocking Luttrell farther down the mountain.

Maybe the Taliban found Axelson and just assumed that Luttrell was also dead. Whatever the reason, the battle space went silent. Other than a broken back, broken shoulder, a broken nose, thighs that felt paralyzed, and a leg he couldn't use, Luttrell was in good shape. Now, at 1:42 p.m. local time, he low-crawled toward the Mark 12 rifle he had dropped earlier while trying to help Axelson. The Taliban didn't know Luttrell's location but began spraying the area where they last saw Luttrell, Axelson, and Murphy. Somehow, Luttrell crawled over a small hill without being seen and spotted a great hiding place nearby: an open ledge in the side of the mountain, surrounded both left and right by large boulders. Luttrell carried no compass, maps, or first-aid kit but knew he could survive here.

Soon, Taliban on the opposite side of the canyon began scouring the terrain they grew up in, looking for him. The Taliban ran up and down the hillside, maybe even competing to see who would be the one to kill the last of the four SEALs.

Later, Luttrell learned that back at the operations center, their commanding officer, Lieutenant Kristensen, took that last cell phone call from Murphy and launched a rescue mission. He ordered the 160th Special Operations Regiment into the same MH-47 helicopter that had delivered Luttrell and the others into the Hindu Kush. A quartet from Team Ten soon joined SEAL Team One buddies James Suh, Shane

Patton, and Dan Healy. Kristensen jumped in at the last minute even though, as commander of the QRF, he could have stayed behind. Eight 160th Special Operations Regiment operators complemented the SEAL teams choppering to the very place where Luttrell, Murphy, Dietz, and Axelson had dropped in. Luttrell was hiding on his ledge about five miles away. During the landing, a Taliban RPG shot through the open ramp and into the fuel tanks, killing everyone on board.

Luttrell knew none of this at the time but did see A-10 Thunderbolts and AG-64 Apache helicopters in the air above him and pointed his rifle into the air, activating the laser as a distress signal that nobody saw. He wondered whether anyone really believed that he was still alive. Despite extreme thirst, he endured. At least the feeling in his legs was coming back. Sunset brought dark shadows, but he could see the glint of an AK-47 followed within seconds by a Taliban warrior wearing a blue and white vest, sleeves rolled up. After another two glints, Luttrell knew he must take action. He minimized the risk of drawing attention to his position by using a suppressor on his Mark 12 rifle, but what happened after Luttrell shot the Taliban between the eyes might have got him killed. The Taliban plunged down a cliff screaming, drawing the attention of two comrades who stared at Luttrell from across the canyon. Luttrell quickly shot them both, hoping that no one heard them fall as the sun set behind the western peaks of the Hindu Kush.

Bleeding, thirsty, and wet, he knew that just as quickly as the locals found the three bodies in the morning, his hiding place might be covered with Taliban. Luttrell could stand up but was thoroughly dehydrated. He had last drunk water nine hours earlier. Somewhere close, there must be a stream down the mountain, but his only chance at all of being rescued would be by helicopter since Taliban warriors occupied the broad valleys below him. Not long after Luttrell started, he tripped and fell some ten feet toward the valley but righted himself and started again, moving sideways to minimize the pain in his legs, making all too much noise snapping the tree branches he used for ladder rungs.

Two hours later, he realized that the Taliban trailed some 200 yards behind him, maybe even using equipment stolen from the Americans. Luttrell didn't have any good options, so he pressed on, hoping to find water and a good place to hide at the top of the canyon. No one in the American aircraft that flew over his head from time to time saw the rescue beacon he pointed upward. The Taliban pursuers came so close that he could hear them talking. Skirting upward and around the mountain, he paused from time to time, looking at the Taliban campfires in the valley below, gradually regaining his confidence one halting step at a time.

He never saw the second fall coming. This time, he seemed to be falling straight down the mountain with nothing to break his fall until a thicket of trees slowed him down. Two hours of painful clawing brought him back up to his starting point—more or less. The hallucinations he began to experience now mimicked what SEALs went through at the very end of Hell Week because of sleep deprivation. Spurred on by thirst, he began hobbling again at six that morning; a well-used trail that he now followed took him past four houses before he turned upward yet again. Luttrell was reciting the Twenty-Third Psalm to himself when he heard the very thing he had been praying for. Just below him somewhere, a brook bubbled—or so he thought.

Several hours earlier back in Texas, the media reported that Luttrell, his reconnaissance team, and the men who tried to rescue him were missing in action. That Tuesday evening, when friends and family gathered at the Luttrell ranch to pay their respects, Luttrell's brother, Morgan, shocked them all by saying that Marcus was still alive. While local law enforcement began a vigil outside the ranch gate, Luttrell, back in the Hindu Kush, leaned out into an exposed position trying to see the brook he could hear somewhere below. The Taliban bullet hit the back of his left thigh, knocking him down the mountainside as the Taliban around him opened up. He rolled, fell, and eventually slowed down enough to crawl downward for some forty-five minutes until he found a boulder that offered good cover.

But now the Taliban completely surrounded him. The enemy scout tracking Luttrell broke into the open, making himself an easy target— just before Luttrell heard something just behind him. Two more Taliban raised their AK-47s five feet away, but Luttrell threw a grenade and ducked behind his boulder, dizzy from the loss of blood but still alive. While watching debris fall from the sky, he pondered his next move.

Team oriented by SEAL training though he was, Luttrell was forced by circumstances to operate solo as a virtual mountain guerrilla, crawling on all fours toward a hissing waterfall, finally reaching the crest; from there, he saw an Afghan village with houses built into a mountainside about a mile below in the welcome silence, like something out of a storybook. And then, he later recalled, Luttrell's left leg gave out just as he began climbing downward; he tried to grab a sapling but tumbled on for 1,000 feet, so far down that there was no choice but to climb 200 feet back up to drink his first water in many hours.

That's when Luttrell noticed three AK-47s pointed at his head. He rolled away from the water and came up with his rifle pointed at the Afghans, but now they spread out and surrounded him. Three more came toward him from a nearby clearing, but no one fired. One exasperated Afghan began screaming, "No Taliban!"

Luttrell knew that this could be a ruse. He might be dead soon, but he was almost past caring. Now he began begging for water, hoping these men weren't Taliban luring him into a trap. The man he later came to call Sarawa seemed to understand. "Hydrate," he said, as Luttrell began to laugh. Later, he learned that the man Luttrell called Sarawa served as the village medic.

A kid brought Luttrell a bottle of water and asked if he was really the guy the village had watched fall down the mountain, while Sarawa and the other adult villagers discussed what to do. Luttrell knew this would not be an easy decision. All these Pashtuns villagers shared blood and culture with the Taliban. On the other hand, a Pashtun tradition called Lokhay (hospitality) dictated that by taking Luttrell in, the village and every man living there guaranteed his safety. Sarawa ordered several men to pick Luttrell up from the ground. Not knowing that the men decided to extend Lokhay, Luttrell pulled the pin on a grenade he carried. The lower level of the houses in this ancient place sheltered goats whose smells and fecal matter permeated everything inside. Most house entrances led down rock stairs to cave-like rooms.

Placed on a cot outside one of the houses, Luttrell put the pin back in the hand grenade he was carrying as Sarawa used a surgical instrument to pull metal shrapnel out of Luttrell's leg to the rhythm of American warplanes passing overhead. A few hours later, villagers carried the wounded American into Sarawa's house.

None of the villagers saw the tattoo until they helped Luttrell change into a fresh shirt. The SEAL Trident on his back prompted one to call him the devil incarnate. That problem went away when the Trident was covered up. Luttrell now told them he was a doctor. That was not true, but he was a medic, with a new name: Dr. Marcus. He stuck with the medic story a few hours later when eight armed Taliban came into his room and beat him up. Since the villagers had taken his rifle into another room earlier, the Taliban didn't kill him. Much to his surprise, when the unarmed village elder told the Taliban to leave at 1:00 a.m., they obeyed him. Within a few minutes, villagers took Luttrell to a hiding place near the river on Thursday, June 30.

June became July, and when it did, the villagers quietly took the American back into the village, surrounded though it was by the Taliban. That night, on the evening of July 1, five days after this mission began, Luttrell met Mohamed Gulab, the resident "police chief" and son of the village elder who had saved him. Gulab told him that a small American base was only two miles away at a village called Monagee.

Looking back, Luttrell now learned that he had walked or crawled about seven miles during what he now called the battle of Murphy's Ridge in honor of his best friend. He began praying to Allah with his visitors as a gesture of respect and gratitude but learned that his presence was a major problem. Since Luttrell could not yet travel, the elder sent someone to the American base at Asadabad, some thirty-five miles away, to arrange a rescue operation.

Gulab told Luttrell about the complex relations between al-Qaeda, the Taliban, and Pashtun villages. He said that both the Taliban and al-Qaeda depended on the Pashtun villages for cooperation yet bullied the Pashtun elders when other tactics didn't work. While the elder traveled to Asadabad, Luttrell's minders moved him late at night to the rooftop of a different house. The next day back at the first house, the SEAL could see Black Hawk UH-60 and MH-40 helicopters looking for someone. The Taliban who beat him up the first night in Sabray (called Salar Ban by some sources) had told him earlier that they shot down a helicopter. Later,

Luttrell learned that many of his SEAL friends had died in it. Gulab said that "Commander Abdul," the local Taliban leader, had demanded that Sabray hand over the American immediately.

Within hours, some of the village kids he had befriended told Luttrell about a parachute carrying a box. Later, they retrieved a radio battery that didn't fit his PRC-148 radio and a Meal, Ready-to-Eat, but at a cost. The Taliban bruised and bloodied most of them. Luttrell tried his radio, not knowing whether he could transmit a signal.

Soon, 1,200-pound bombs dropped on Taliban positions several miles away, causing collateral structural damage to at least one village wall and blowing off several thatched roofs but otherwise leaving Sabray intact. Although Gulab reassured him that most of the village was willing to fight the Taliban if necessary, they both knew that Luttrell needed to leave the village—and soon. Since Asadabad was at least a two-day hike, Monagee, on the other side of a steeply dangerous mountain but only two miles away, was the only viable option. They started at about 11:00 that night in the darkness since lanterns might alert the Taliban to their position. Thunderstorms hit the mountain later above them that evening, creating virtual rivers racing between the houses in Sabray. Lightning followed, delaying Luttrell's July 2 escape.

Back in East Texas at about that time, even as the media discounted the possibility that any of the SEALs might have survived, SEAL Senior Chief Petty Officer Chris Gothro remained optimistic. Earlier messages from Luttrell convinced many in SPECWARCOM that he might still be alive. He was, but Luttrell knew that the time window for him to escape from the Taliban might soon close. The next morning, Luttrell sat looking at the mountainside looming between him and safety when Gulab ran up to him from out of nowhere. "Run, Dr. Marcus, run," Gulab shouted while dragging the SEAL to his feet for a run to a hiding place in the lower part of the village. Within minutes, Gulab had brought Luttrell's rifle and seventy-five rounds of ammunition, everything that Luttrell now carried. Gulab carried his own AK-47. "We fight, Dr. Marcus, we fight," he said in an affirmation of Pashtun tradition honored for at least 2,000 years even as the Taliban combed through in the upper village.

Gulab covered the door while Luttrell covered the only window after they shoved two cushions behind the door, just as gunfire above them on the mountainside began. The Taliban fired at random in the air to terrorize the villagers into revealing where the SEAL could be found. During the forty-five minutes of silence that followed, they finally reached the house where Luttrell hid. At 10:00 local time on the morning of July 3, Luttrell left the hiding place, rushing 200 yards to a flat field, but Gulab soon guided him to a blackberry bush on a hillside. From there, Luttrell spotted the target that cost his three SEAL teammates their lives on a ridge behind them. Ahmad Shah, a forty-something local leader loosely affiliated with the Taliban, wore a red vest, black turban, and red-flecked beard. Shah seemed to be staring right at Luttrell, but Luttrell couldn't shoot him without endangering the village. Shah could do nothing either since Gulab was the oldest son of Sabray's top village elder.

Within a few minutes, Gulab and Shah walked up the mountain calmly talking as if friends for life. Luttrell worried and wondered if he was going to be surrendered and executed on the spot. Hand over the American, or every member of your family will be killed—that was the handwritten message that Shah gave Gulab moments later before storming away with his army, surrounded by Sabray villagers armed and ready to defend the single SEAL.

Two men from the village now helped Luttrell struggle up some nearby rock steps. Much to his surprise, an Afghan Special Forces warrior and two U.S. Army Rangers joined them. They moved him up the hill to a goat pen where an Army Corpsman began treating his wounds with antiseptic and fresh bandages as more Rangers arrived. Luttrell explained the danger all around them over tea, warning that the Taliban force was probably watching their every move. He showed them notes he had kept, identifying exactly where the Taliban surrounding the twenty Americans probably lurked. Luttrell thought that as many as 200 Taliban surrounded them despite later, lower estimates from other sources. The Americans went back to the second safe house where they waited for rescue after nightfall as village kids surrounded and hugged Luttrell.

A helicopter coming from somewhere nearby at about 10:00 that night prompted Taliban lights across the face of a nearby mountain—

Taliban lights that American fighter bombers and helicopters soon darkened. Later, Luttrell learned that at least thirty-two Taliban and al-Qaeda had died in the firestorm. Within minutes, Luttrell clambered into the American helicopter with Gulab holding on to Luttrell's arm, far from eager to take his first flight but willing to go. The unlit village lingered briefly below them and then faded away.

Later at Asadabad, Luttrell and Gulab said their last good-byes. Gulab could not return to his village, so he began helping the Americans. Luttrell wrote his memoir, *Lone Survivor*, with Patrick Robinson, which has been relied on for much of this account. But now, six days and four hours after the mission had begun, Luttrell stepped off a C-130 at Bagram, thinking about three heroes named Danny Dietz, Matthew Axelson, and Michael Patrick Murphy.

CHAPTER TWELVE

The Hornet's Nest

ADAM BROWN BLEW OUT THE CANDLES AND GLANCED OVER AT HIS KIDS laughing a few feet away. He turned thirty-six today but had only thirty-five days to live. After a quick family photograph with his wife Kelly and children Nathan and Savannah, he hurried to eastern Afghanistan, arriving at the DEVGRU compound on Monday, March 1, 2010, as the frequency and pace of SEAL missions increased. And now a new target, code-named "Objective Lake James," a Taliban leader deep in the Pech River valley of Kunar province, meant yet another helicopter ride.

Michael Cardenaz, a twenty-nine-year-old Army sergeant, the most recent American victim of Lake James, had died ten days earlier. Brown finished his third mission there on March 15 and called home via Skype at 3:15 a.m. Afghan time. Early on St. Patrick's Day, two mornings later, Brown was talking basketball with another SEAL Team Six member. They were surrounded by good stuff from home—a flat-screen television, couches, and even a high-quality espresso machine—when they learned about the next mission.

This would be a "direct action"—a short-duration strike carried out in a hostile environment using special military capabilities and, often, classified operational techniques. Such direct actions dated back at least to World War II when the Allies conducted sabotage missions and delivered Norwegian soldiers specially trained by the British special operations executive to destinations behind German lines. During the intervening years before 9/11, Americans conducted direct-action missions during the 1994 Rwandan genocide and in Bosnia three years later.

This 2010 SEAL mission resembled others conducted by the U.S. Special Operations Command. The operation began with a review of available intelligence, including images and known infiltration routes. The high-value target was in an extremely dangerous valley commanding Taliban forces that earlier had killed a number of Army operators at a forward operating base (FOB) in the area. Back home in Arkansas, Brown's son Nathan woke up on the morning of St. Patrick's Day worrying about his father.

That night just after sunset, Brown and the rest of the SEAL Team Six team began their brief work commute in MH-47 helicopters. Earlier, snipers in lead helicopters hugging steep Taliban-infested hills and ridges had angled through the treetops. The pilots squinted down through dust-covered windshields, hoping to find a decent landing zone among the rocky, far-too-close jagged rocks. Faced with few options, the pilots flew away to make a second pass before finding a place where the SEALs and others could fast-rope down into unfriendly territory. The team included several Afghan special force warriors and U.S. infantrymen, all struggling to focus their night-vision goggles on the boulder-filled ground around them.

After two hours fording streams and negotiating cliffs, the Afghans began slowing down even though they carried only half as much gear as the Americans. Three hours into the mission, one of them laid down to rest, saying he couldn't go on. Brown picked the Afghan up, pushing him forward on the craggy trail. Within a few minutes, they stumbled into several tightly closed huts. The SEALs searched the single hut whose owner willingly opened the door for them, finding no weapons but warning a seven-member family to stay inside. Six hours after the assault force roped in, the snipers led the way to an assembly area near to the place where Objective Lake James lived. The terrain was so rugged that one SEAL later estimated he had fallen down at least fifteen times, part of the reason the operation was running two hours late. When interviewed several years later, an Army sergeant said that Brown and other members of the assault team invaded a hornet's nest, sneaking past hard-core Taliban, attacking the queen bee, and knowing but accepting that if the operation didn't go right, they might be swarmed by Taliban as well.

They split up, moving down both sides of the rut that passed for the main street, passing some houses so far down an adjacent hill that the SEALs could have stepped on the roofs. All was quiet—intelligence, surveillance, and reconnaissance (ISR), called "eyes in the sky," confirmed that everyone in the village was sleeping. Everyone sleeping here, as far as the eye could see, from the ridge where the operation force was walking and all the way down to the valley floor about a quarter of a mile below, sympathized with the Taliban. The road (if you could call it that) veered sharply left, revealing seemingly identical buildings and huts on the other side of the widening valley just before the Objective Lake James compound, the width of two basketball courts and containing two structures surrounded by eight-foot walls, came into view. Prior intelligence surveys revealed two structures inside. The residence beneath a mountain hugged the western-most wall.

The primary SEAL assault team moved into position as Brown covered the eastern wall. SEAL Heath Robinson could see from his vantage point atop the southern wall that a man sitting on the residence porch heard something and picked up his AK-47.

The guard aimed at Heath, but Heath quietly dropped him a second later, making no more noise than a staple gun. A second fighter high above the northwestern corner of the compound heard the round and sprayed a few AK-47 rounds into the darkness before the SEALs knocked down that fighter and a third Taliban inside the courtyard. Soon, five women emerged from the house and moved together toward the dead Taliban in the courtyard, wailing as they pulled an ammunition pack from his chest and crying even louder as they spread out to the other two bodies.

Heath knew the routine. The Afghan interpreter tried his best to coax the women into putting their hands up in surrender, even as one of them pulled an AK-47 from beneath her robe and began waving it around, her finger on the trigger, moving away from the other four women, who remained on the porch, surrounded by as many children.

Heath now watched a Taliban fighter carrying a pistol emerge from the house and crouch next to the children while darting across the porch to another door on the opposite side. Moments later, the woman told the SEALs that no one was left inside. We're just simple farmers, one of the women said, just before the gunfire coming from elsewhere in the village descended on the compound from points nearby, soon joined by intermittent fire from inside a house they thought was empty.

Five minutes after the operation inside the compound began, the team learned from ISR that the surrounding area was quickly coming alive, with unidentified individuals converging toward and surrounding the American forces. Worse yet, a Taliban shooter peered from a window inside the residence, but none of the SEALs could get close enough to take him out. Thinking out loud, Heath said that a 40-mm grenade fired from a grenade launcher might solve the problem. Brown volunteered—again. He had joined the Navy twelve years earlier, convincing recruiters to ignore his troubled past of thievery to support a serious cocaine habit. By age thirty-three, Brown had lost the vision in his right eye during a battle, broken his back and one of his legs, but talked his way into training and a tryout for SEAL Team Six anyway. He overcame his blinded right eye to become a sniper and the only person with such a record to become a DEVGRU operator. Heath knew all this, so he was not surprised to hear Brown volunteer and watched him move into action. Brown climbed up the eastern wall to survey the bare ground leading to a gate on the left and the residence in the far distance.

Brown now picked his path to the target. A wall about four feet high extended toward a tree in the middle of the courtyard, within grenade-launching distance of the house now sheltering the Taliban sniper. Brown slowly lowered himself onto the foot-wide fence, inched toward the tree, and tried to get a clear shot at the sniper through the heavy tree branches before the gunfire began. And it wasn't coming from the house. A shooter in the barn, silent until now, began firing at Brown, who was soon struck in both legs; worse yet, he became tangled in tree branches and couldn't roll off the wall in time to duck. A second volley now struck Brown's left side between his armor plates as the sniper in the house created a cross fire pinning Brown down. Three SEALs, Heath Robinson, Craig Vickers, and Rick Martinez, instantly went into action. Heath poured fire over Brown into the barn as Craig jumped onto the barn roof toward a spot from which he could throw a grenade; before he could, a bullet struck his wrist. In the meantime, two SEALs somehow pulled Brown out of the tree branches and off the wall, dragging Brown toward the courtyard gate and relative safety. And as they did, despite his wound, Kraig climbed back onto the barn roof to launch a grenade.

The Taliban courtyard went silent as the assault force medic began cutting armor away to get a closer look at Brown's severe wound as grenades exploded nearby. "I'm okay," Brown said, as everybody around him looked down, knowing better. The team strapped him to a litter, radioed for help, and hustled as quickly as they could to an emergency landing zone, stopping every twenty yards so that the medic could do chest compressions as bullets zipped everywhere. One man helping with the litter fell headlong into a ditch, and another was shot in the bicep as they hurried down the valley through farm terraces in the darkness. Despite exhaustion, nobody slowed down. Since Brown survived so many previous injuries, some thought he might survive despite the severity of his wounds, but he died a few minutes after being carried aboard the rescue helicopter.

Brown was posthumously awarded the Silver Star for Conspicuous Gallantry the next year. Eric Blehm wrote the story of this brave SEAL in *Fearless*, which this writer largely relied on for this chapter.

CHAPTER THIRTEEN

The Streets of Ramadi

Kevin Lacz was a new guy in the Al Anbar province of western Iraq, joining Task Unit Bruiser, Charlie Platoon, SEAL Team Three, surrounded in 2006 by a hostile and bitter population most of which only tolerated the Americans. Lacz wrote his memoir *The Last Punisher* with Ethan E. Rocke and Linsey Lacz about nine years later, but his descriptions are as fresh as today, in no large part due to the contemporary journal he kept during those tumultuous times. Lacz wrote of Ramadi at a time when that city of some 300,000 souls was occupied by ISIS forces hostile to America and its allies. "Muj hunting" is what the SEALs called the missions to find and neutralize the mujahideen fighters of Al Anbar province who were doing everything they could to kill Americans.

One of the favorite "Muj" targets in 2006 was Camp Blue Diamond, a U.S. Marine base on the northwestern side of Ramadi, just to the east of the SEAL "shark base" across the Euphrates River. This time, the Muj came as swimmers, or so someone told the SEALs running to the roof of "shark house," where the SEALs slept—when they could. Most of the men who assembled atop shark house wore only undershorts. Lacz chuckled at the appearance of this motley crew, then focused his night-vision goggles on some motion barely detectable across the river. Lacz himself let some 150 rounds fly as one of twenty SEALs who brought the mujahideen operation to a quick and deadly halt.

Kevin Lacz grew up in middle Connecticut; excelled in baseball, soccer, and even golf; but gave them all up due to boredom before joining his high school swim team. At James Madison University in Harrisonburg, Virginia, he majored in rugby, girls, and booze until planes slammed into the World Trade Center buildings on 9/11. That morning, he watched the attack on television at the rugby team house just after waking up. He soon learned that Bruce Eagleson, a close family friend back in Connecticut, escaped but returned to the burning buildings to help others and never came out. During the memorial service for Eagleson, Lacz decided to become part of the American forces who would avenge the World Trade Center, following his grandfather and great uncle into the U.S. Navy.

An old poster at the Navy recruiting station featuring mustachioed frogmen emerging from the water quickly convinced him a few days later to become a SEAL. After basic training and sixteen weeks of hospital corpsman training, he arrived at Coronado Island, six miles south of downtown San Diego, California. Lacz insisted in his memoir that Navy SEALs are born, not made, with two things in common, namely, drive and resilience, traits sharpened during BUD/S training. Two weeks later, the United States invaded Iraq, but Lacz suffered a back injury and was held back, joining Class 246 after his recovery. Then he was off to jump school at Fort Benning, Georgia, followed by a four-month SEAL Qualification Training in February 2004. That course has since been expanded to twenty-six weeks.

SEAL Qualification Training provides SEALs training in mission planning, intelligence gathering, land/sea navigation, and boat operations, among other skills. In July 2004, after more medical corpsman training, Lacz returned to the West Coast for his new assignment with SEAL Team Three, much of which now deployed to Iraq.

Chris Kyle, already known as "The Legend" for his record as a SEAL sniper in Iraq, returned to Team Three in April 2005. And Kyle gave Lacz the nickname that stuck with him during his SEAL career. Since he slightly resembled a character on the 1990s television sitcom *Coach*, Lacz became "Dauber." After a sixty-day Army Sniper School tour at Fort Benning, Lacz returned to Charlie Platoon, just in time for predeployment training. Four years after joining the Navy, Dauber Lacz was on his way to combat in Iraq.

The C-17 taking Charlie Platoon into six months of combat lifted off from Naval Air Station North Island that April 2006 morning. They stopped at Bangor, Maine, and Spangdahlem, Germany, for refueling before dropping into Al Taqaddam, Iraq, after some sixteen hours of flight time. While in Germany briefly, Lacz and the others learned that they faced service in one of the most dangerous destinations in the world. He wondered how combat might change him. When Lacz boarded a helicopter at Al Taqaddam for the brief flight to Camp Ramadi, he thought about that day less than a year earlier, in June 2005, when sixteen men, including a pilot from Connecticut, died trying to rescue Marcus Luttrell of *Lone Survivor* fame.

They arrived in Iraq safely, but Lacz, as one of the newest guys in Charlie Platoon, promptly started convoy duty on Route Michigan, a dangerous transportation artery that became a major draw for insurgents planting improvised explosive devices (IEDs). Route Michigan begins in Baghdad, runs into the desert in a westerly direction through Fallujah into the main street of Ramadi, and turns into the desert. Humvees, seven-ton trucks, and tractors snaked slowly along the road, everyone on board intensely wary of the danger around and even under them. There was every reason to be cautious. Route Michigan was then the Iraqi "Mother Road" of IEDs planted to kill Americans and erode their will to win one bomb at a time.

In Ramadi, Lacz and the others faced a garbage-filled four-lane highway with many side streets blocked by American barriers and vehicles blown up in prior attacks. Front-seat passengers watched constantly for loose wires, plastic bags, or fresh dirt, all signs of an IED that could kill everyone in a truck or Jeep. Sometimes, the insurgents simply cut holes in the floorboards of their aged, rusting cars and dropped the IEDs into the road. During the year before Lacz arrived, virtually every American convoy suffered at least one IED attack. Some U.S. Marines came to believe that when Iraqi villagers walked around outside, no IEDs had recently been buried on the street.

Day 4 started quietly enough, but a new posting at the mission planning hut told the SEALs that the missions would begin at midnight. The briefing began at 2:00 that afternoon. Surrounded by buddies nicknamed

Chucky, Spaz, Rex, and Squirrel, Lacz learned that the platoon would be going after a known bomb maker in a nearby village called Tamim, riding in M1152 cargo troop carriers bearing names like Snake Eyes, Cobra, and Shipwreck. Lacz carried rosary beads and $200 in cash just in case he got separated from the others. All told, he shouldered fifty pounds of gear and medic equipment onto his assigned truck. Big Zev was named for a similar truck appearing in a television series about Vietnam. Before going to Tamim, they picked up the Iraqi Security Forces Special Mission Platoon (Jundis) that the SEALs were training. Many Jundis showed strong loyalty again and again; others joined simply to get a job, but a few carried mujahideen sympathies, so the Jundis learned the mission details at the very last minute if at all. Officially, the Jundis trained to take over the fight against the insurgents. However, the SEALs did all the heavy lifting. This particularly lethargic, unprepared Jundi platoon was rousted out of bunks and forced onto the trucks. Their interpreter, known only as "Moose," a highly skilled former Jordanian Special Forces operator, worked on a contract basis.

The Muj target reportedly rested in a compound consisting of several houses within a walled enclosure. The plan called for the Jundis to silently climb the compound wall, open the gate for the SEALs, and stand aside for the SEALs to conduct the search and find the target. Instead, the Jundis let their AK-47s loudly slap the compound wall as they climbed, announcing their arrival to the insurgents inside.

Lacz heard the gate latch open and peered into a garage only about ten feet away as the Jundis stepped to the side, hugging the compound wall and letting the Americans burst through the front door. Lacz cleared the first room himself and followed others into a dirty kitchen where a woman and several children stood screaming. Lacz pushed them into a corner as other SEALs moved past into a room filled with mattresses and prayer rugs. Two rooms later, they found and handcuffed two unarmed terrorists. On the way out, Lacz discovered that he had conducted the operation with an empty rifle. "Not bad, but not great," one of the veterans said to Lacz back on Big Zev, whatever that meant.

Two weeks into the Ramadi deployment, Lacz tired of training mostly ambivalent Jundis for operations they didn't want to conduct.

Charlie Platoon, now self-labeled as "Punishers" in honor of a Marvel Comic character, redeployed to Camp Corregidor, a FOB in the Ma' Laab district of southeastern Ramadi, to support a major Army offensive in the works. The seven-mile night trip along the Michigan Route under a starless sky took them past some of the taller buildings in Ramadi, some of which Lacz studied from his gun turret in the lead vehicle, thinking about possible sniping positions.

"Holy shit," he said to himself as they passed the crater-pocked wire-strewn intersection of roads the Americans called Michigan and Sunset Streets. Oddly enough, the lead vehicle offered the most protection that day since the insurgents, for whatever reason, typically didn't choose to hit the first truck or Jeep. But now they passed Government Center, a modern, three-story brown building with a damaged two-story central tower in downtown Ramadi, an insurgent magnet, surrounded by rooftops providing abundant shelter for snipers. U.S. Marines did some serious damage here, but now, in late April 2006, the Punisher platoon really didn't know who was watching them pass the Government Center in the darkness.

The small-arms fire that Lacz heard in the distance kept him alert to possible ambush at any moment. IEDs going off probably meant that a Marine or Army brother just died or was injured a few miles away. The smell of feces running in the open sewers permeated everything.

Corregidor loomed as a black hulk in the darkness but opened its gates for the newbies. The Punishers quickly worked out a relationship with their host, the U.S. Army. This meant trimming hair and beards to regulation standards and staying out of the way while awaiting action orders. After a few days, Lacz made friends with "Brown," an Army sniper in his early thirties with eight months of in-country experience. The next day, after checking the whiteboard at the operations tent for any assignments, Lacz inspected a possible sniper position that Brown had told him about. The pockmarked guard tower was rocketed and machine-gunned many times but offered a good view down many of the nearby alleys where insurgents might lurk.

The chief petty officer to whom Lacz now reported offered only one piece of advice: get some. He quickly found the spiral staircase upward, joining two Army guys on guard duty. After a quick briefing from one of the soldiers, Lacz knew the insurgents were savvy enough to present few easily identifiable targets. Finally, after two hours behind the scope, at about 4:00 p.m., he spotted a man staring toward Corregidor. He was covered by "moon dust," the American nickname for the gritty Iraqi dirt that stuck to everyone who went outdoors there. The potential target wearing a blue shirt, black pants, and leather sandals was about 300 yards away. The man disappeared behind a wall but moments later peeked out from a doorway with something bulky in his arms. It was an AK-47.

That was all that Lacz needed under the current rules of engagement. No civilians walked near enough to the insurgent to worry about. He calmly focused between the man's shoulders, tracked him, and squeezed the trigger of his MK 11; within a split second, the target dropped, to rise no more. The Army guys laughed and cheered as Lacz began looking through his scope for a second target. Several men, waving white handkerchiefs in the air, retrieved the insurgent later but left the AK-47 in the dust. This was week 2 in country for Lacz.

Abu Musab al-Zarqawi launched al-Qaeda forces the day that Lacz arrived, attacking American positions all over Ramadi, beginning with a yellow dump truck full of explosives positioned at an Army observation post. Two years earlier, Zarqawi had personally decapitated American contractor Nick Berg on camera.

Now, in late April 2006, the SEAL Punisher Platoon would work in direct support of the 502nd Infantry Regiment, 1st Battalion, as forward observers and snipers. Lacz teamed up with six Jundis, three other SEALs, and his new Army buddy Brown for a quick trip to a soccer stadium about two miles away. Their convoy paused several times to draw out any insurgents targeting them before stopping in front of the soccer stadium long enough for the eleven-man team to get out of the Army trucks and into crouching positions behind cover. Surrounded by broken glass and trash, the Punishers listened to the Army Cougar infantry mobility vehicles drive away, leaving them in silence for about ten minutes. Then their operation began with a "soft knock" at a house sporting a rooftop with good overwatch potential. The owner, who instinctively knew he had no choice, welcomed the Americans inside.

After darkening the house, the SEALs knocked a hole in the wall surrounding the house as quietly as they could, even though the insurgents and their sympathizers probably knew exactly where they walked. Earlier, Brown had alerted the team to one of the insurgents' favorite tactics: lobbing grenades onto the rooftops of houses where Americans positioned themselves.

They listened to eastern Ramadi come alive for prayers at 6:15 a.m. the next morning just before several men got out of a large black car some 200 yards away and began staring upward at the American position, making no effort to conceal themselves. Since these suspected insurgents carried no guns, all Lacz and the other SEALs could do was watch them, at least for now. Eventually, the men piled back into the black car and left.

There was nothing below the SEALs on their rooftop to see until they spotted some hostiles hiding outside of rifle range sneaking behind a wall near the soccer stadium. While listening to other SEALs on the far side of the stadium begin a firefight, Brown's team called in Hellfire missiles on the Taliban hiding behind the wall, even as small-arms fire began to pepper their position.

Shortly after 8:30 a.m., Humvees and Bradley fighting vehicles began arriving near their position, but, the QRF couldn't get close enough to their building for a quick evacuation. The SEALs would have to carry their gear from one covered position to the next for at least 300 yards, leapfrogging from wall to wall. The first 200 yards was uneventful, but then the real action began at an intersection. AK-47 fire began hitting all around them, edging ever closer. Lacz could see the shooter in an alley and began returning fire as the team ran for the vehicles some 100 yards or more away.

Lacz lacked personal experience with IEDs until early May 2006; that morning, someone rushed into an Army chow hall during breakfast and began begging everybody there to drop everything and become stretcher bearers. Lacz, a trained Special Operations medic, could do this and more. He ran for the field hospital a few yards away with one other SEAL medic. All too soon, a severely wounded American occupied his assigned duty bed.

Crash carts, electrocardiogram monitors, intravenous fluid stations, and even solar blankets were being rushed in. Young but experienced Army medics prepared to treat the wounded, their faces wearing earlier tragedies seen all too often. This place became chaos within minutes, treating Marines from a Marine convoy ambushed by insurgents who rigged a string of 155-mm artillery shells to explode in a killing zone. Lacz watched the maimed and dead Marines flood in, planning payback for so much blood, so many men dead or dying. Lacz went instinctively to the "ABC" formula he had memorized for situations just like this: air, breathing, and circulation.

All too quickly, the beds began to fill. The Marine assigned to Lacz was young, blond, and mortally wounded (or so it appeared), suffering with a massive head wound. Lacz never learned whether that Marine survived, but he returned to his tent a few hours later with new resolve. A major mission rolled a few weeks later. An insurgent bomb maker in southwestern Ramadi was targeted for action. This would be an early morning operation targeting a compound of houses deep in insurgent friendly territory. A platoon of eighteen SEALs accompanied by twelve Iraqis started the forty-five-minute trip to the objective at about 2:00 a.m., hoping to be back in camp before dawn.

Lacz and the others moved cautiously through the targeted compound, avoiding contact with low-hanging electrical wires that seemed to be everywhere in maneuvers becoming all too routine. A strip charge, about the size of a baseball wrapped in camouflage, blew the door off before the SEALs moved through the dirt and debris into the first house and on to the second. The Iraqis collected the women and children, then searched for cell phones, computers, and software, in the first house and followed the Americans to the second.

They fully expected a gunfight with insurgents in the third house but instead found a herd of goats on the roof—maybe placed there to mock the SEALs. The insurgent bomb maker was nowhere to be found. Lacz and the others, loading computers and cell phones onto trucks, looked up to see a city bus lurching around the corner. Instead of commuters going to work, this bus carried mujahideen warriors. Several insurgents who charged out of the bus promptly became butchered meat as .50-mm machine guns tore the bus into shreds. After that, the SEALs rode back home to the shark base in silence.

The next target loomed north of Ramadi beyond the Euphrates River. Lacz would serve as point man in yet another raid on a compound. The team covered all the escape routes from the compound from four different positions as Lacz positioned a ladder against an eight-foot wall. He easily climbed over and took his first step on the other side of the wall onto the ground only to feel his left foot punctured by an eight-inch nail. He looked down at the point on the nail through his night-vision glasses while muffling obscenities. Seconds later, he removed it and hobbled toward the house fifty yards away with eight SEALs and four Jundis. They crept into place, the strip charge was placed on the door, and the detonation man pushed the button at the exact second an identical charge exploded one house away, but nothing happened.

The explosives man, known as Squirrel, knew instinctively why the strip charge didn't detonate. The firing device jarred loose during the jump down the backside of the wall into the compound. Squirrel quickly dug into his bag of explosive goodies, coming up with another firing device twenty seconds later. Maybe this one would work.

And it did. Lacz and his teammate Chris Kyle sprang toward the building half a football field away and then walked through the jagged doorway where the door stood seconds ago. This second effort might mean trouble for Lacz and others on the other side of the doorway; he knocked down an old man obstructing the doorway while holding his hands in the air, breaking the man's nose. Worse yet, one of the Jundis accidentally fired off a round that nearly struck Lacz and another SEAL. Lacz climbed into their truck a few minutes later, feeling very lucky to be alive.

Mid-June found Lacz and his crew working twenty-four- to forty-eight-hour sniper overwatch operations when not conducting direct-action missions against specific targets. One day in mid-June while getting ready for some bunk time after seven days of operations, Lacz and his platoon went back into action to rescue a kidnap victim of al-Qaeda in Iraq (AQI). The son of the Ramadi police chief was being held in a house with no compound wall. Unless this mission succeeded, the five well-armed young AQI fighters might decapitate him during a propaganda video.

An abandoned school 200 yards to the west and another building 300 yards to the south provided good staging points for the combined force operation with several Iraqi Special Forces. Lacz noticed that the Iraqi Special Forces guys didn't dress any better than the SEALs. Some wore disheveled chocolate chip–patterned camouflage uniforms, sporting green helmets; others wore black helmets, and one guy called Akmed sported a Hooters bandanna. Duct-taped flashlights adorned their rifles.

Chris Kyle, two other SEALs, and several other American troops set up sniper and machine gun positions in the southern building just before Lacz and the assault team crashed through the door and quickly moved up to the roof. The ground team found all five fighters, the kidnap victim, and the family who lived there asleep. Kyle noticed that the Iraqi Special Forces team was getting better.

Uneventful though it was, the daring raid brought the Punisher Platoon plenty of new freelance work around Ramadi for both the Army and the Marines. They delivered the Punisher product—a one-two punch of combined sniper overwatch and direct operations—with particular skill and efficiency. The Punishers became the talk of the town among the American forces as the "clear" segment of the "clear, hold, build" doctrine espoused by General David Petraeus.

The Marines established Observation Post Firecracker in the heart of central Ramadi at a four-way intersection just north of Government Center—or what was left of it. Muj insurgents became increasingly aggressive in the early months of 2006, and the jarheads now asked for sniper services. The SEALs set up an overwatch operation 200 yards from the intersection and began doing foot patrols along the streets, watching mongrel dogs scour rotting trash for food. One of the first SEAL targets was a corner house that turned out to be "Muj central," filled with hostile women.

The SEALs watched Muj suspects come and go for hours before taking action. Lacz set up a sniper position in a room facing west toward the Firecracker observation post. He gathered pillows from around the house, put together a shooting platform facing the window, removed some steel bars that restricted his view outside, and waited for action.

Oddly enough, nobody was coming out of the house for prayers. Cars began driving slowly by as military-age men scouted the SEALs overwatch from a distance. Still, all was quiet until an RPG slammed into the wall near one of the other SEAL positions, close enough to give Lacz ringing ears for hours. Worse yet, machine gun fire began pelting the window in front of him. Lacz dove for cover just as his was covered with bullets. Yet another RPG arrived, hitting but not crashing through Lacz's window. Ten minutes later, all was silence as Lacz began to think about the deadly forces around him. He thought back to a sign he had seen somewhere when he first arrived in Iraq saying "Complacency kills" and resolved not to be among its victims.

In late June, the Marines asked for sniper support again in a mission storming Ramadi General Hospital, which AQI had turned into a fortress earlier, violating all rules of war. Lacz and several other SEALs would conduct a sniper overwatch mission from just north of the hospital. Camp Hurricane Point, a Marine base at the confluence of the Euphrates River and the Habbaniyah Canal in northwestern Ramadi, served as the launch point for the fifteen-minute boat ride through mosquito-infested swamp water. The insertion point, filled with vegetation and tall, thick reeds, reminded Lacz of pictures he had seen of the Mekong Delta in Vietnam.

Their first mission that day was reconnoitering a compound that might become a staging area for the eventual assault on Ramadi General Hospital. Three big buildings sat within the compound walls about forty yards from the water's edge. Squirrel, the explosives guy in the Punisher Platoon, led them over the wall and into the compound. All three of the three-story structures were empty. Better yet, two were air-conditioned. While Chris Kyle took first watch, Lacz snoozed.

Kyle watched Ramadi arise for Morning Prayer at 6:00 a.m. Two hours later, some five Muj fighters, dressed in Adidas track suits, jumped out of tall grass for potshots at Marines across the Euphrates River. The SEAL snipers marveled at their luck, watched the Muj begin setting up a mortar, and waited for all five to stand up at the same time. When they did, a SEAL M79 grenade launcher and rifle fire put all five insurgents down—permanently.

Later that day, a SEAL called Jonny (not Johnny) who also served as a medic, shot a Muj warrior pushing a wheelbarrow full of bomb-making materials into the SEAL-occupied compound, and then tried to save the dying man's life. Although the Marines began their assault on Ramadi General that morning, the SEAL Punishers saw no more action that day. They delivered "Bernie" the dead Iraqi to Ramadi General Hospital, now occupied by U.S. Marines, the following morning.

The Army requested Navy SEALs' help again in mid-July for an American push into south-central Ramadi to establish a command observation post (COP) in yet another residential compound at the intersection of two dusty, garbage-strewn streets that the Americans designated Sunset and Baseline Road. Lacz and the SEAL Punisher Platoon would serve as the main reconnaissance team. Once again, a Marine boat crew would drop the SEALs at the insertion point on the Habbaniyah Canal.

They boated into south-central Ramadi, got out by a grove of trees, and fanned out across a narrow perimeter to establish security before moving out single file toward the compound. As they slowly approached a canal full of raw sewage, Lacz, back in the middle of the column, saw a hand signal to freeze, followed several seconds later by three rifle shots. As he walked forward onto a flimsy, narrow bridge, he saw a skinny Muj on his back. Most of his face was gone, leaving only his teeth, nose, and eyes. An AK-47 was next to the putrefying body. One of the SEALs shot the Muj again before they all crossed the narrow, flimsy bridge, walking toward the rendezvous compound.

Lacz could see it, a football field away, surrounded by an eight-foot wall. The SEALs quickly spread out for security as two of their number climbed over and quickly opened the gate. Inside the large house, they searched empty rooms but quickly moved to the rooftop to overwatch enemy movement in every direction. Soon, they moved on to an even better spot atop a four-story apartment complex, knocked holes in the rooftop walls, and then waited for action through the night.

In the stillness of an early morning, Lacz spotted a man sporting a thin beard and a small, crude bag. The man turned toward the SEALs and shifted forward to ease the load, confirming what Kyle and Lacz already knew: he was hiding a 155-mm artillery round that could take out a tank. Within a few seconds, they watched the middle-aged man move toward the middle of the street, crouch, and place the IED in a small hole and then look up toward them. "Dump him," Kyle said. Lacz did just that, knocking the insurgent down in a second. Later, Lacz theorized that the Muj knew that they couldn't stop the American offensive into Ramadi by direct attacks, so they settled on IED tactics to disable American patrols. Kyle took down some ten Muj that afternoon against a singleton for Lacz, who hoped for better luck after sundown. At 6:00 a.m., Lacz spotted a man in standard Muj uniform consisting of black track pants and a T-shirt peaking upward around a corner at the SEAL position with a cell phone in his hand, making him a legitimate target. That kill was the last of twenty-three confirmed SEAL kills from the rooftop that day.

The first recorded American sniper killed British General Simon Frazer during the Battle of Saratoga on October 7, 1779, from a distance of about 400 yards. The first sniper school was established during the Vietnam War. And now Ramadi was sniper ground.

Lacz later described that city as a large, long game of Whac-A-Mole in districts heavily populated by Muj insurgents who were usually easy to identify. The hardest part of the daily routine was safely getting from their home at the shark base to COP Falcon. Once established in mid-July 2006, COP Falcon grew from a single compound to a complex with its own parking lot, becoming a base of operations for an initiative driving toward the Al Hawz and Al Mualemeen districts of southwestern Ramadi, clearing and holding all territory along the way.

The wide, dusty paths that Americans designated Sunset Boulevard, Route Michigan, and Baseline Road became prime spots for insurgent attacks. The Army combat engineers spent endless hours dealing with deadly explosives dropped by the dozens, trying to keep the operational status of American supply routes "green" as the Army recovered several dead Americans from a smoldering tank destroyed during an insurgent attack with Lacz providing sniper overwatch.

A few days later, Lacz and Kyle began sniping in style again—from an air-conditioned, ground-level bedroom surrounded by pillows. From that vantage point, they watched two men on a moped (small motorcycle) casually drop an IED in the middle of Sunset Boulevard and motor toward them. Chris "The Legend" Kyle opened fire when the Muj came within about 200 yards, dropping them both with one bullet. Some of the Muj, motivated by money rather than Mohammed, could earn $200 for digging an IED crater and twice as much for dropping one. This motivated many a poor Iraqi to become an IED "dropper."

Lacz was back at the shark base settling into sleep one night when somebody brought a new mission into the tent. A high-value target—probably a known bomb maker—was spotted in northern Ramadi. Minutes later, several American trucks, most carrying turret gunners, pulled out of the compound. Twenty-five minutes later, they pulled into a poorly lit neighborhood and down a long alley surrounded by high walls. This didn't look good to Lacz, but direct-action missions like this seldom became child's play. This one could be a two-for-one: two targets, one to the left and one to the right, hit at the very same time by two different columns within the team. Lacz now spotted a military-age Muj suspect while leading the right column to the place where they would go over the wall. Lacz discovered that the front door, which was supposed to be right in front of him, was on the opposite side of the house. There was nothing to be done but adjust since nine men loomed inside the target compound. Lacz gave the signal to move out but within seconds was knocked down by a blast that might have killed him had Lacz been a few feet closer to the door. The charge was detonated thanks to a mix-up in hand signals. Lacz quickly recovered and led his part of the team inside through a long hallway and up some stairs toward the rooftop, where they quickly cuffed three very hostile Muj suspects.

Intel was right this time. The house was stuffed with bomb-making material. Just as they loaded the bad guys into a Humvee for questioning, an American .50-caliber machine gun opened up on someone in the darkness nearby. Some eight would-be ambushers positioned themselves about a football field and a first down away from the SEALs, not knowing that airborne ISR spotted them. Within seconds, all of the Muj exploded into pieces as the convoy backed out of the dead-end alley.

Soon, the SEALs began getting daytime assignments on the streets of Ramadi rather than conducting nighttime sniping operations from rooftops. The idea was to draw heavy Muj insurgent fire and then call in Army reinforcements to destroy the threat.

Squirrel was point man one morning just about a month after they arrived at COP Falcon; they strolled down K Street near a mosque, passing a huge pile of trash, when Lacz spotted the barrel of a PKC Soviet machine gun aimed right at them just as ten rounds screamed into their exposed lines. A second PKC opened up on them from a mosque some 150 yards away as the SEALs sought what protection they could from nearby telephone poles. They must find a building from which to return fire and fast, even as still another squad of Muj began firing into them from a third position behind the SEALs.

They spotted a likely building more than forty yards away. Lacz stepped on the chest of another SEAL who lost his balance and fell backward onto the ground as Lacz burst through the front door.

Bounding up the stairs and onto the rooftop, Lacz began scouting the street fight below as a second SEAL squad, some 150 yards away, also came under fire, but soon the SEALs suppressed all the Muj action on K Street and sauntered back to COP Falcon.

Later that month, after a single IED killed four Marines in Ramadi north of Baseline Road, Charlie Platoon conducted yet another sniper overwatch operation from yet another four-story apartment building. Now sarcastically called "The Legend" by his buddies, Chris Kyle led the dual column, comprised of sixteen SEALs, two explosives experts, and six Iraqi Special Forces operators, out of COP Falcon an hour before midnight, weaving left and right through houses and huts clustered together to a destination about two miles away, navigating dark streets and shadowy alleys, any of which could have been hiding Muj ambushers.

They reached the apartment complex three hours after leaving COP Falcon. Muj insurgents saw them but waited until noon the next day to launch rocket grenades and pepper the SEALs with machine gun fire.

Thirty minutes later, the insurgent attack ended as quickly as it began. But the Muj weren't finished with the SEALs.

One of the explosives experts spotted the 155-mm artillery round booby trap propped against the front door at the very last minute—just before the SEALS began the return trip to COP Falcon. The bomb was apparently planted during RPG and machine gun fire attack earlier that afternoon. Soon, it would be midnight, and the Muj looked everywhere for them. After breaking through the wall separating them from the rooftop of an adjacent building and reviving a SEAL who fell twenty feet off the adjoining roof, the Punishers gently and quietly maneuvered a quarter block of the explosive C-4 down from the fourth floor onto the artillery shell leaning against the front door and escaped through the market streets. Five minutes later, the five-minute timer on the C-4 exploded back at the apartment building door. Back at COP Falcon within a few hours, the Punishers enjoyed a few laughs about fooling the Muj.

Late that July, elements of SEAL Team Eight then in Baghdad joined the Punishers in Ramadi for the launch of a new tactic: some SEALs would conduct overwatch while other SEALs conducted walking patrols designed to lure the Muj insurgents into revealing themselves. The sniper element set up shop in a building not far from the last one but with a 360-degree view of the area where the SEAL ground patrols would soon be operating. Shortly after 11:00 the next morning, the ground patrol paraded down K Street, soon drawing AK-47 fire and grenades from the Muj fighters. Lacz raised an American flag he carried on every operation over the sniper position, drawing insurgent fire and giving the ground patrol enough time to seek cover in a building.

COP Falcon began even more intense missions in early August 2006 as the Americans fought a war of attrition against the insurgency, even as IED casualties increased. The Army launched an operation surrounding and searching a targeted area in Ramadi north of Baseline Road inch by inch and house by house.

Charlie Platoon, still sporting their Punisher helmets, moved out at dawn on August 2 with a few SEAL Team Eight snipers. Ten Jundis came along to help clear structures and detain occupants back in the neighborhood where the Punishers had narrowly avoided being blown up by an artillery shell two weeks earlier. Despite the danger everywhere, Lacz recalled later that there was no place else in the world he would rather be that dawn.

Everything looked green in the darkness viewed through the infrared lasers on their rifles and night-vision goggles. The dual columns merged into one north of Baseline Road and then split into squads as necessary to search individual buildings and establish sniper overwatch positions. Their Jundi team hardened into good troops thanks to four months of solid operational experience and intensive SEAL training. Army operators established blocking positions all around the targeted area, using Bradley Fighting Vehicles and Abrams tanks. The searches became almost routine—starting with a soft knock, following with quick but thorough searches of every room, and ending with the confiscation of any war material they found. The first few searches that morning produced little opposition, at least until small-arms fire could be heard in the distance.

"Biggles is down," said another SEAL on the radio, prompting Lacz to run up a flight of stairs to the rooftop for a better overwatch position: they couldn't see anything but heard a SEAL machine gunner later identified as Marc Lee providing more than 100 rounds of covering fire, even as a Bradley Fighting Vehicle was ordered in to medevac Ron "Biggles" Job out. When Biggles left, several Jundis joined the First Squad, which would be leading everyone back to COP Falcon. On the way, Lacz put down a Muj who had sprung out of an alley, following that with a grenade meant for any other Muj behind the first one.

The squads leapfrogged back to COP Falcon, jogging when they could and masking their movements from time to time with smoke grenades on the two-mile trek. Resting briefly at the SEAL house, they learned that Biggles was alive but on his way to a hospital in Germany. It was time for more payback. Chris Kyle learned that the intelligence gurus had identified the building from which the Muj shooters targeted Biggles. His buddies loaded up grenades and magazines for a run back into the fire zone that very day.

The SEAL Team Three operators listened to the plan with a mixture of fury and cynicism. The Airborne Rangers in the Tactical Operations

Center decided on an old-style frontal assault, deployed in Bradley Fighting Vehicles, which just happened to be outside ready to go, late on the morning of August 2. Heavy metal tunes, such as Metallica's "Seek and Destroy," blared as they bounced along toward the mission. Tanks would soften up the Muj with a heavy barrage of 25-mm cannon fire just before the combined forces, once again led by SEALs, jumped out of the Bradleys and back into action.

The Bradleys in which the team rode added to the artillery medley during the short trip back into danger. The targeted compound still smoldered as the Americans assaulted the first two-story structure, clearing one room at a time until two unarmed Muj fighters sprung up and tried unsuccessfully to fist fight their way out. Seconds later, both Muj hugged the dirty floor looking up, their hands flex-cuffed.

And with that, the squads moved on to another two-story structure far enough away that the assault team got back into the Bradleys. The smoke was so thick this time that the Bradley cannon's 25-mm barrage hit a car instead of the building door. Lacz quickly kicked it down and cleared the first two rooms on the ground floor.

Lacz was clearing rooms on the second floor when Muj machine gun fire tore open a window in the downstairs hallway, fatally wounding his friend, fellow SEAL Marc Lee. Back at the shark base in Camp Ramadi at 5:00 p.m., while the mortuary team prepared Lee's body for the return home, Lacz agreed to be part of the SEAL honor guard.

Two weeks later, with Marc Lee dead and Biggles blinded for life, Kevin Lacz was looking for more payback. Finally, just days before the fifth anniversary of 9/11, a good assignment came in. The "hide" was a three-story building not far from where Marc Lee scored his first kill with a good view toward "Muj country" to the east. Lacz selected a sniping window that gave him a 1,000-meter (half-mile) view of all arterial roads into the targeted area. Yet he didn't expect a Muj insurgent to be walking around so boldly, an AK-47 in his right hand, about 766 yards away at 8:00 a.m. Mr. Muj offered a challenging yet feasible target: payback for Lee and Biggles. The Muj was clueless, exposed as he was, smoking a cigarette and standing next to several unarmed buddies. Lacz let his training take over, breathed slowly, focused into the morning light, squeezed the trigger slowly, and watched, without any remorse, the Muj die.

Lacz smelled the cordite around him as he tucked the empty shell casing into his shirt pocket next to the Rosary. His partner, Squirrel, smiled slightly and began scanning the horizon for his own next target. Machine gun fire peppered another SEAL sniper position a few minutes later, but there was no visible target to kill.

Mid-September found the SEAL shark base at Camp Ramadi quiet as Chris Kyle and other SEALs began returning to the United States. "The Legend" killed 101 Muj insurgents by Lacz's count, representing at least half of Charlie Platoon's total. The trip from Anbar to Al Taqaddam Air Base about thirty miles away through IED-infested roads to see Kyle off hardly bothered Lacz that day, in sharp contrast to the anxieties of his first days in country. Lacz and many of the others would be leaving in about two weeks.

Soon, Lacz and some of the others returned to the shark base. When not on duty, they held makeshift fishing poles over the timeless Euphrates hoping for tugs on the line that might remind them of home while swigging whiskey that was not supposed to be there.

Mike Monsoor of the SEAL Team Three Delta Platoon was supposed to go home too. On Friday, September 29, Monsoor and the rest of Delta Platoon went on one last sniper overwatch mission, killed two Muj fighters, but then came under a heavy assault. On a rooftop scanning for targets, Monsoor felt something hit his chest, looked down at a hand grenade, fell on it, and sacrificed himself, saving several SEALs and Iraqi soldiers. He died thirty minutes later, becoming the first Navy SEAL in Iraq to be awarded the Medal of Honor. He also received a posthumous Silver Star for saving a fellow SEAL from intense enemy fire five months before he died.

Lacz went on to portray himself in the Clint Eastwood film *American Sniper*, spending time with Bradley Cooper, who portrayed his friend Chris Kyle. Some ten years after his experiences with Chris Kyle, Marc Lee, and many others, Lacz said that he had never felt more alive than during those days with the Punishers of Charlie Platoon on the streets of Ramadi.

CHAPTER FOURTEEN

Enemy Central

MATT BISONETTE HATED DOING BOOK REPORTS AS A KID. YET HE found his career in junior high school while reading *Men in Green Faces*, an account of SEAL missions in the Mekong Delta of Vietnam by Gene Wentz. Some ten years later, he became a SEAL, serving from 1998 to 2012, and as "Mark Owen" wrote *No Easy Day*, an autobiography covering some of the best-known and most obscure missions of the Navy SEALs. Bisonette served on many unusual missions in Afghanistan, Africa, Iraq, and Pakistan, but rescuing a merchant ship from pirates might have been the most challenging.

He began training for SEAL Team Six (DEVGRU), which tracked down war criminals and conducted rescue missions in 2004, as part of a nine-month selection process called the Green Team. Six years earlier, he had passed BUD/S training and thus was already a SEAL, joining SEAL Team Six to advance his career. The course included the arduous physical training most would expect but also focused on close-quarters battle, taught at a special "kill house" with hallways and rooms where this close-in tradecraft could be practiced again and again.

Bisonette wondered whether the kill house training might be any easier than thirty days jumping out of planes from high altitudes over Arizona. He negotiated and navigated his way through the rooms, clearing "bad guy" targets and letting "good guys" go, while six instructors watched him from a catwalk just below the ceiling. He focused entirely on getting through the course.

After his initial SEAL training, Bisonette deployed to Iraq in 2003 and stayed part of the following year before beginning DEVGRU training. One of the things that Bisonette liked best about DEVGRU was the "tool kit" of rifles and guns customized with individualized grips and triggers available to the team. Five years later, Bisonette and some of the other DEVGRU SEALs faced pirates who had just seized an American ship—the first such seizure since 1815.

Bisonette saw the news report on Wednesday, April 8, 2009, while waiting to board a flight from California to Virginia Beach, Virginia. *Maersk Alabama*, owned by Maersk Line Limited, a squat 17,000-metric-ton blue and red container ship launched in Taiwan eleven years earlier, badly needed a paint job. The pirates fled *Alabama* in one of the lifeboats, using Captain Richard Phillips as a hostage. Bisonette watched in real time from the airport lounge, wondering whether his own SEAL Team would be called in to assault the orange sixteen-footer bobbing in the surf just off the Somalian coast. USS *Bainbridge*, a guided missile destroyer whose namesake, Commodore William Bainbridge, commanded USS *Constitution* in the War of 1812, shadowed the lifeboat. Just as he expected, Bisonette learned within minutes that the DEVGRUs would travel to Somalia.

The operation began Thursday morning shortly after the pirates phoned in a $2 million ransom demand for Phillips. Twenty hours later, a C-17 ramp opened over East Africa to drop several high-speed assault craft with their crews into the water, just over the horizon from USS *Bainbridge*.

A communications specialist and two other support team members joined them that day. While Bisonette and his team slept in the plane, *Bainbridge* Captain Frank Castellano offered to tow the pirates anywhere they wanted to go, providing food and water along the way. During one of the catered deliveries, pirate Abduhl Wal-i-musi asked for some first-aid treatment. Soon, Musi was eating ice cream and drinking soda on the stern of *Bainbridge* in full view of his three comrades. When Musi's new best friend, a Navy SEAL named Gary, asked Musi if he would mind the *Bainbridge* towing the pirate boat a little closer, Musi agreed, not realizing that this sealed his comrades' fate.

Soon, the pirate riding on top of the boat canopy became an easy target, as did the second man visible behind the steering wheel. Yet nothing could be done until the third pirate showed himself for fear that Phillips might be killed. And so they waited. Finally, on Sunday, April 12, the third pirate appeared in the rear hatch of *Alabama*'s lifeboat, oblivious to the SEALs' snipers, and when he did, three shots rang out in the darkness. Two of the SEALs' snipers sped down the towline.

Bisonette arrived too late for the *Alabama* operation, but several months later, in the central mountains of Afghanistan, he watched eight insurgents escape from a targeted compound. These "squirters" ran toward a ridgeline some 329 yards away; since Bisonette was not yet acclimated to the high altitude and lugged more than eighty pounds of guns and gear, he struggled to keep up.

Just as suddenly as the squirters reached the crest of the distant ridge, they turned to fight the SEALs. Bisonette dropped one carrying a PKM machine gun just as his teammates dropped two more. The five surviving squirters may have believed themselves safe after crossing the ridge and beginning the descent into a valley, but a drone pilot spotted them. Close air support provided by an AC-130 gunship weighed into the fight, killing or wounding most and leaving a few for Bisonette and Phil to track down and kill. Bisonette and his team paused long enough on the ridge to make sure that three insurgents wearing black cheetahs, sneakers, and baggy shirts were really dead.

A squirter RPG landed a few feet away, temporarily deafening Bisonette's buddy "Phil" (not his real name) just minutes earlier. Phil tracked one squirter to a compound, even as Bisonette and the others tracked another one who had set up an ambush point in a ditch, using hand grenades to finish him off. Bisonette stepped inadvertently on a dead squirter before stripping him of an AK-47 and an Individual Integrated Fighting Systems chest rack invented for the SEALs during the Vietnam War. An RPG that Bisonette had found that day featured prominently in a SEAL photograph display that evening back in Jalalabad. Back in Alaska, Bisonette's parents remained proud but worried.

They never wanted him to enlist in the military. After all, he had been accepted for college in California. And so, at his father's insistence,

Bisonette earned a college degree before signing up and intended to become an officer, but, rightly or wrongly, a former SEAL convinced him that enlisted SEALs saw more action. Bisonette marked his eleventh combat deployment in 2009. Almost all his deployments took him to Afghanistan. That summer, the annual Taliban offensive started right on schedule. An American who went missing in late June appeared in a video less than a month later. That very night, Bisonette and his team briefed into the operation. Navy intelligence suggested that Private First Class Beaudry Robert "Bowe" Bergdahl was being held south of Kabul. The team would land just far enough from the suspected location to be out of RPG firing range for an operation at sunrise the next morning. They launched at midnight in the worst of all possible circumstances: under a full moon on a cloudless night.

The CH-47 dropped them in an open field with no cover at all about an hour and a half later, immediately drawing machine gun fire from the Taliban in a house nearby. While tracers gradually came ever closer to the helicopter behind them, Bisonette and the rest of the team ran for the Taliban house; a SEAL popped up between rounds, pulled out his "pirate gun" (a single-shot M79 grenade launcher), and put a round inside the door, giving the rest of the team just enough time to clear the house without civilian casualties, taking out several Taliban while Bisonette watched other insurgents some 329 yards away flee the fight. Two Taliban fled on mopeds.

Bisonette and the two snipers pursued the minibikers while another SEAL and the dog team chased other Taliban who might lead them to Bergdahl. Bisonette's team spotted the mopeds parked by a road just after nearly stepping on and then shooting an insurgent hiding in tall grass. Two more popped up about 300 yards away behind a hay bale, prompting one of the snipers to climb a nearby incline for a better view. Bisonette's team was limited to a very narrow space on the opposite side of the hay bale protecting the insurgent. Bisonette raced around the bale with a grenade in his hand as quietly as possible, but when he was about thirty-three yards away, the Taliban popped up. Before Bisonette could even duck, two SEAL snipers knocked the Taliban over with machine gun fire, igniting an RPG rocket and turning the Taliban into a human firecracker.

They never found the other moped driver or Bergdahl, but in the search that day, one of the combat assault dogs was killed, and Bisonette's buddy Phil was seriously wounded.

Two months later, Bisonette and his eight-man SEAL Team Six crew choppered into Kunar, one of the hottest zones in eastern Afghanistan. The Army FOB commander and first sergeant briefed them in a small room filled with maps, antennas, and cheap plywood furniture, surrounded by sandbags, placed to keep mortar rounds and RPG rockets out. This part of the lower Hindu Kush was filled with perfect ambush spots, caves for insurgent operations, and good access for supplies and material.

Nearby loomed the northwestern frontier province of Pakistan, which had once been a British colonial province and was now in some respects independent of the national Pakistani government. The Americans called Kunar, the Afghani province that bordered Pakistan, "Enemy Central" because it served as a rendezvous point for the Taliban, al-Qaeda, and independent mujahideen forces in the insurgency.

Now, Bisonette and his crew prepared to kill or capture several leading Taliban conducting a strategy meeting south of this FOB just three weeks before their scheduled return home. Minutes after getting out of the CH-47 Chinook chopper, while Bisonette relieved himself, tracer rounds and rockets began showering in, some coming within ten feet of the SEALs. American .50-caliber machine guns and mortars responded from all sides of the FOB as Bisonette and the others ran through the darkness and in through the gate. Later, during the briefing, the commander explained that this happened about once a week, but Bisonette saw an opportunity to get some payback for Phil and the dead assault dog.

Soon, Bisonette and the others watched Taliban patrols around the suspected compound on television monitors fed by drones circling above the target, knowing that this operation against larger forces might be a serious challenge. The SEALs would traverse a ridgeline above the Taliban, hoping not to be detected as two other American teams patrolled the main road into the targeted valley, pushing the targeted patrol uphill toward Bisonette's crew. Previous experience suggested that the Taliban might at some point simply scatter, running for tree lines and adjoining valleys.

Bisonette and his team sported much longer hair than their Army counterparts, not to mention mismatched uniforms, making quite an impression as they began the mission that night, following a goat trail up into the mountains. Their destination was a potential kill zone looking down at the insurgents. Within minutes, they thought of a better idea. The SEALs would trail behind an Army patrol of some twenty soldiers and then quickly sneak into the targeted area, hoping that anyone following the Americans might be far enough behind not to notice.

After the early morning Army patrol began, the SEALs quickly split off, following a road that narrowed and ended. Three hours later, they spotted the stone and mud buildings where the Taliban and other insurgents supposedly gathered. Although drone pilots saw patrols all around them, the team saw only one option: they must get off the road and move upward through the trees, hoping to find sniper observation points above the target compounds before the night brought impenetrable darkness.

Two hours later, they found the upper reaches of the very goat trail that the team first planned to follow and squeezed against the ridgeline, winding upward on a path seldom more than a foot wide, clinging to high cliffs and staring at deadly drops into the valley below.

The path ended abruptly at a near perfect view of three buildings and smaller structures on the edges of the target compound; this wouldn't be a static watch for targets from sniping positions. Instead, they would search the entire compound. Snipers providing overwatch from one of the roofs scanned a nearby creek for any signals of sentries as Bisonette and some of the others began searching for insurgents from building to building.

Moving through the compound, the SEALs killed two targets in the first building as Bisonette spotted a Taliban escaping from the second structure, barely reaching a window before he too was cut down. Bisonette now heard the support team on the ridge behind the compound begin neutralizing Taliban guards in at least three firefights, picking off five insurgent fighters, even as an AC-130 gunship could be heard positioning to take out others trying to escape northward.

He now began searching an adjoining alley with another SEAL, making his way through wet clothing on lines and assorted junk, using their laser scopes to see what or who was ahead. His SEAL partner Charlie opened up on one insurgent, saving Bisonette as Bisonette watched the man crumple only an arm's length ahead. The compound was clear of Taliban. Bisonette was a very lucky man who now regretted leaving his body armor behind as they began "cover-your-ass" procedures to justify killing the insurgents.

They photographed the weapons collected and inventoried documents, computers, and thumbnail drives collected while AC-130s above them continued pummeling insurgents only a few hundred yards away in darkness that would soon become sunrise. All told, seventeen insurgents died that morning, without a single American casualty. During the helicopter ride back to Jalalabad four hours later, Bisonette couldn't remember an operation that had gone down so perfectly.

CHAPTER FIFTEEN

The Three Killings of Osama bin Laden

IN THE EARLY SPRING OF 2011, WHILE BISONETTE WAS BACK IN VIR-
ginia Beach, he learned from his yard man, of all people, that Bisonette's
SEAL boss, Jay (not his real name), had just left for Washington, D.C.,
on something big. The Arab Spring began the previous December with
the self-immolation of a protester whose merchandise was confiscated by
a municipal inspector in Tunisia. Unrest quickly spread to Libya, Syria,
and even the Horn of Africa. During "kill house" refresher training and
target practice, Bisonette noticed that Jay was missing and wondered why.
The very day he returned to Virginia Beach from training, Bisonette and
several others arrived at the SEAL command headquarters for a meeting. The next morning, a Friday, they went to a secure conference room,
requiring special badges for entry. This time, no photographs or maps
covered the wall next to the four flat-screen TVs. Almost thirty people
waited to start, but not Bisonette's boss, Jay. A briefer told the Green
Team crew to pack their usual assault gear for a joint readiness exercise
in North Carolina but couldn't say more. This time, no "new guys" carried
the gear for more senior Green Team members. While they packed, several of Bisonette's buddies guessed that the destination was Libya, Syria,
or even Iran. One even claimed that they were going after bin Laden
again—as others laughed and snickered.

During Bisonette's sixth SEAL deployment in 2007 to CIA FOB
Chapman in Khost province, the team rushed to Jalalabad, Afghanistan,
on thinly sourced news that bin Laden was in Tora Bora. Bisonette spent

almost a week with the Pakistani military on the Pakistan–Afghanistan border at a checkpoint while his teammates searched nearby mountains looking for the "man in the white robes." Bin Laden never surfaced during the weeklong mission.

Now, in 2011, Bisonette arrived in North Carolina a day late on Tuesday due to some prescheduled commitments he couldn't cancel. The training site in the deep piney woods consisted of two concrete two-story buildings. One of the guys who arrived earlier told him that bin Laden was supposedly located in Pakistan. Maps of Pakistan and a place called Abbottabad filled the walls of a nearby conference room. Bin Laden lived, or so sources said, in a city of 1.5 million souls named for Major James Abbott, who had founded the town as a district headquarters of the British colonial government in January 1853.

The team consisted of twenty-eight Americans, an interpreter, and a combat assault dog. Two helicopters designated Chalk One and Chalk Two would provide transportation for the mission. The chalk designation practice went back to World War II when during the invasion of Europe, invasion organizers scribbled aircraft flight numbers on soldiers' backs. The target compound consisted of a large building and a smaller guesthouse. Bisonette and his team would be covering the guesthouse. This disappointed Bisonette since bin Laden was thought to be living in the larger structure. However disappointed, Bisonette studied a model mock-up of the target compound centered on a five- by five-foot plywood platform, sporting details down to small trees positioned in exactitude. The one-acre complex hugged a residential neighborhood not far from the Pakistani equivalent of West Point. Kakul Road ran east to west along the north side of the $1 million estate, whose high walls blocked the public views of the first story. American intelligence called bin Laden "the Pacer" since he paced around a garden courtyard in the compound. The CIA watched him for months, using highly sensitive eavesdropping equipment and cameras behind glass-mirrored windows in a nearby rental property on high ground.

The key to finding bin Laden was Ahmed Al-Kuwaitee, who served as one of two couriers for the terrorist. The CIA identified Kuwaitee as early as 2002, began efforts to find him immediately, but did not locate him until about 2010. Eventually, they traced a white truck that Kuwaitee used from time to time back on to the compound on Kakul Road in Abbottabad.

Kuwaitee was the chief courier between bin Laden and Ayman Zawahiri, leader of al-Qaeda. The key to finding Kuwaitee was Khalid Sheikh Mohammed, the very terrorist who conceived and planned the first World Trade Center attack in 1993 and later suggested using commercial airlines as offensive weapons. Captured in early March 2003, Khalid identified Kuwaitee as bin Laden's main courier; by September 2010, the CIA followed him to the bin Laden compound at Abbottabad. Everything they knew suggested that bin Laden lived on the third floor of the main building with two wives and as many as a dozen children.

While the entire team studied the models, briefers told them that Bisonette's team would secure the guesthouse occupied by Kuwaitee and his family while a second team crept to a door on the south side of the larger building and climbed a spiral staircase to the target living quarters. The third assault team would patrol the compound exterior and deal with any squirters who attempted to escape the complex as well as police and any military forces that saw the SEAL assault and responded. Toward the end of the one-hour briefing, bin Laden became "Geronimo" for operational purposes.

When Bisonette and his team began working out the operational details, they immediately saw a problem. Since there was nowhere in the residential neighborhood adjoining the targeted complex for the helicopters to land, they decided to rope in from above, covered by two snipers. The doors would be blown open by foot-long explosive charges with strips of adhesive to help positioning.

Despite all this planning, the assault option was not yet green-lighted by the White House, which was still considering several viable alternatives, most notably including a bomb strike leveling the house. Such an air strike would eliminate the need for ground troops and avoid the risks of the disastrous late April 1980 Eagle Claw operation to rescue American hostages in Iran. However, the risk of collateral damage to civilians was very high, and the probability of positively identifying bin Laden after dropping thirty-two smart bombs at the compound was very low.

While the higher-ups pondered the risks, Bisonette and his teammates waited and watched Geronimo pacing around his compound in real time. Often, a child walked with him. From time to time, military helicopters flew directly over the compound toward the Pakistani military academy, suggesting that the SEAL helicopter attack, if authorized, would not surprise the compound guards. The assault team had practiced the operation at the replica compound in the piney woods of North Carolina for three days, making the initial phases "routine," even though the building interiors still remained a complete mystery. For planning purposes, the team assumed that Geronimo, Kuwaitee, and two others would be armed; the SEALs waited to be sent in soon.

Instead, they went home for the weekend.

The "dress rehearsal" the following Thursday began in an airplane hangar with the pilots, SEALs, and other participants briefing the Chairman of the Joint Chiefs of Staff and the commander of the Special Operations Command on how the operation would be conducted. Later that evening, the VIPs, now wearing night-vision goggles, watched fully armed assaulters drop into the mock compound.

The following Sunday, April 24, Bisonette checked in with the rest of the Virginia Beach assault team members for the flight to Jalalabad not knowing whether the mission was a "go." They all traveled light. Bisonette carried a few changes of clothing, a shaving kit, and some flip-flops as he watched his friends wish their families a happy Easter. Bisonette had already checked in with his parents by cell phone as he drove into the base. The C-17 Globemaster, stuffed to the top with everything they needed, roared down the runway. During the flight, helicopter crews, National Security Agency analysts, and CIA spooks all kept to themselves. Many SEALs picked places to hang hammocks or plop down on the floor in air mattresses for the nine-hour flight to Germany. Another eight hours in the air would put them into Bagram Airfield about twenty-five miles north of Kabul and 233 miles east of Abbottabad. A CIA analyst named Jen sitting next to Bisonette told him that she began tracking bin Laden since she joined "the Company" right after college. Bisonette heard something similar before the 2007 raid that went nowhere. He wondered whether maybe, just maybe, this time the CIA might be right.

Right on schedule, they bounced into Jalalabad in the darkness; for many of the SEALs, Jalalabad was already a second home. Will, a self-taught Arabic-speaking SEAL already on base when they arrived, now joined the assault team. He marveled at the target compound mock-up hidden from view behind padlocked doors.

Bisonette spent the rest of that day checking and rechecking his gear, testing the batteries in his night-vision goggles and laser sights three times. The second evening, the mixed-service assault team joked around about whether Brad Pitt or George Clooney would star in the Hollywood version of this mission. Bisonette traded barbs with the helicopter crews he knew from previous operations with the 160th Special Operations Aviation Regiment. Many assumed out loud that their success might guarantee President Obama's reelection. Day 3 brought inoperable cloud cover and more briefings in a narrow room packed to capacity. Drone footage, satellite photographs, and PowerPoints on flat-screen TVs filled the hours as they waited for the politicos to give the final green light. While they waited, the politicos created an appropriate cover story just in case the mission failed or somebody fell into Pakistani hands. The public was told that this was a search-and-recovery mission looking for a downed drone—a tall tale that even the most casual observer would see through as soon as the first journalist learned that twenty-two SEALs, an interpreter, and an assault dog waited for them in Pakistan.

Later, they learned that President Obama had signed off on a mission the next night.

Twelve hours before zero hour, Bisonette rolled out of his bunk—sleep deprived but ready to go late that afternoon after scrambled eggs, pineapple, and ham washed down with orange juice. He slapped on a desert camouflage uniform with ten cargo pockets but no sleeves. Like most SEAL Team Three members, his pockets bulged with batteries, PowerBars, knives, ammunition, and a radio. Bisonette also carried $200 in American greenbacks for buying rides and bribing Afghanis—if it came to that. Special night-vision goggles gave him a viewing radius of 120 degrees, three times wider than regular-issue equipment.

They started the mission at sundown, piling into dusty old buses moving toward the hangars filled with Black Hawk helicopters ready to fly. Bisonette would be leading a team of SEALs fast-roping off the helicopters and into the compound—at least that's how it was supposed to go down. Bisonette double-checked the safety on his rifle just before the abrupt liftoff. A few minutes later, they flew into Pakistani airspace. Bisonette slept almost until the choppers reached the drop point.

The SEAL Team Three crew grabbed for anything they could hold on to as the Black Hawk bobbed up and down in a rough hover over the target and suddenly turned onto its side, as Bisonette remembered it, slipping toward the ground with Bisonette's legs hanging outside the half-opened door. All he could think about was how much this was going to hurt. Bisonette always assumed that if he died in action, it would be in a gunfight, not in a helicopter crash. They went into the compound nose first, coming to an abrupt halt, leaving them all hanging in midair, six feet above the ground. The tail end of the Black Hawk was caught in the twelve-foot privacy wall, just high enough to keep the main rotors spinning.

Bisonette and the rest of the direct-action team dropped to the ground, inside instead of outside the walls as was planned, about ten minutes behind schedule, but nobody was hurt despite the crash. Only a locked gate stood between them and the main compound. Bisonette cleared a prayer room nearby as somebody else blew open a gate, even as the second helicopter dropped other SEALs outside the wall, but things continued to go wrong. Bisonette's team tried to break through the metal covered guesthouse door. Worse still, adjoining windows protected by narrow vertical metal bars resisted many sledgehammer blows. The second team discovered, after blowing their way through the compound wall, that a second barrier loomed between them and the main building.

Now, five minutes into the assault, AK-47 rounds began landing just above their heads, covering Bisonette's shoulders with glass. Bisonette closed in on the guesthouse, yelling all the time for Ahmed Al-Kuwaitee, bin Laden's most trusted courier, to surrender while shooting into the house from those few windows they could poke their rifle barrels through.

A woman trailed by three small children and carrying a baby soon opened the guesthouse front door and told them Kuwaitee was dead—and he was, ten minutes into the mission, as they moved toward the duplex where bin Laden was supposed to be living on the third floor. The SEALs also killed Ahmed Al-Kuwaitee's brother, Abrar, living on the other side of the duplex along with his wife, according to Bisonette's account. They now searched for bin Laden, working their way through some chicken coops. An explosive charge opened the door between the SEALs and some tile stairs leading upward into the quiet darkness.

Often, SEALs started this type of assault with flash grenades, but tonight would be different. On the second-floor landing, using his night-vision goggles, Bisonette could see a large corridor leading toward a porch along the south side of the structure. They cleared four doors before moving up the stairs toward the target, knowing that as many as four armed men waited, hoping to ambush a SEAL. A beardless man quickly peeked around the corner but didn't open fire. The SEALs assumed him to be Khalid bin Laden, a son of the notorious al-Qaeda leader. His second darting glance around the corner was his last. Now there was one man left. Bisonette peered through the greenish tinge of his night-vision glasses for anyone else blocking the path upward, quietly moving up one step at a time behind the point man, halfway through the thirty-minute mission. The third-floor landing closely resembled the floor plan just below it.

Somebody there quickly peered out from one of the doorways about ten feet down the hall, drawing two quick, silent shots from Bisonette's point man as women and children somewhere in front of the SEALs wailed. Quietly and quickly looking around the corner into the room, Bisonette saw two women in long robes stooping over a figure leaking brains out of a bullet wound on the right side of his head. The man on the floor twitched until Bisonette and another assaulter shot him in the chest. While Bisonette searched a small but well-organized office just across the hallway, he heard someone say that the third floor was secure.

All in a night's work.

President Obama and others listened and waited, but the SEALs slowed down long enough to go through the checklists, comparing the corpse to composite drawings and photographs, after verifying that he was six foot, four inches tall, just like the terrorist Osama bin Laden. One of the SEALs began treating the target's fifth wife, who had suffered a leg wound from a ricocheting bullet. Others began taking DNA samples from the dead man. Bisonette noticed that bin Laden seemed much younger than he imagined. His hair didn't have a speck of gray. They squirted water on his face, cleaned it with a blanket to ensure they wouldn't miss anything, and then took some high-quality photographs while listening to someone on the second floor say on the radio that help was needed there to gather documents and computers. The sensitive-site exploitation was nearly as important as killing bin Laden. Someone held the target's eyes open for a better photograph. Down on the second floor at the same time, a team bagged well-organized notebooks, papers, flash drives, videos, memory cards, computers, and other data as other SEALs carefully watched the women and children on the balcony. The lead CIA interpreter and security operators outside the compound walls dealt with pesky neighbors.

An order to destroy the downed Black Hawk helicopter, misunderstood in the confusion, prompted the demolition team to place explosives around the main house. Finally, someone noticed and corrected the mistake just in time.

Extracting the crew from the downed Black Hawk presented yet another difficult challenge. The pilot climbed down using a rope instead of making the six-foot jump. The SEAL tasked with destroying the Black Hawk then began placing charges around the fuselage, climbing up to the tail and working down, assisted by an Army explosives ordnance device technician, knowing that the debris could collapse at any time.

Back on the third floor, getting a blood sample from bin Laden proved surprisingly difficult since two spring-loaded syringes wouldn't properly fire. Eventually, the SEALs gave up, hoping that two saliva samples might confirm the identity. The women out on the balcony refused to identify bin Laden other than to call him "the sheikh," but a young girl finally identified the corpse by name. One of the SEALs now shamed the women into admitting the truth and sent a message to President Obama and Secretary of State Hillary Clinton: "For God and country, I pass Geronimo—Geronimo ekia." The "enemy killed in action" bumped his way down three flights of stairs headfirst as his women wailed. Bisonette did the last search of bin Laden's small office before moving on to a wooden dresser nearby. In sharp contrast to the rest of the apartment except the study, bin Laden's dresser could have passed Marine boot camp inspection, with T-shirts folded and squared. Nearby, clothes hung in precise intervals. Bisonette discovered bin Laden's AK-47 and Makarov pistol both unloaded, indicating unlike other men in the compound, that he was unwilling to fight for his family.

Even though SEALs throughout the compound begged for more time, the mission commander barked, "Post assault, five minutes!" over the radio, telling everyone in military shorthand to be at the landing zone in five minutes. Bisonette followed the trail of blood from bin Laden's body down three flights of stairs, up and over Khalid's body. Outside, he noticed that the women and children had huddled in a corner of the courtyard as far away from the crashed helicopter as possible. Bisonette didn't know that the Black Hawk and C-47 helicopters sent to pick them up were running out of fuel.

Bisonette joined his Black Hawk group while other SEALs exited the compound on the C-47 chopper. Bisonette and other SEALs carried bin Laden to the incoming Black Hawk over a recently plowed field, threw the corpse in, and climbed aboard. Had the C-47 approached when scheduled, it would have been blown out of the air by the explosion. Instead, the C-47 landed safely near the south wall of the compound with just enough fuel for the return flight. Bisonette stared at the red blinking fuel warning light on the pilot's instrument panel as the helicopter struggled into the air. Seconds later, Bisonette heard the Black Hawk leaning against the wall inside the compound explode as his own helicopter circled the scene; one of the other SEALs was sitting on top of bin Laden since there wasn't any room elsewhere.

Soon, Bisonette's Black Hawk dropped back to the ground, yards from a second C-47, surrounded by SEALs with weapons pointed outward. Several SEALs sitting next to Bisonette jumped out to lighten the load as Army fueling specialists dragged a gas line toward his Black Hawk, refueled it, and jumped back on the second C-47. Bisonette's Black Hawk and the C-47 refueling helicopter lifted off together for the forty-five-minute trip back to Jalalabad. On the way, Bisonette thought about all of the possible intelligence left behind in the rush to get the mission done before the Pakistani military arrived on the scene. The second-floor hallway bulged with stacks of boxes that could have been searched, not to mention desk drawers still unopened.

Back at base, while carrying the body bag, an Army first sergeant handed him a 75th Ranger Regiment commemorative coin, telling Bisonette that he would be his son's hero for the rest of his life. Nearby, a hangar in Jalalabad bristled with Navy brass. "Let's see him," one officer said, prompting Bisonette to drag the body bag out of the chopper and onto the cement floor. The body was decomposing but still recognizable. Just to make sure, Admiral William McRaven ordered a six-foot-four SEAL nearby to get down next to the corpse. As McRaven nodded, Bisonette noticed Jen, the CIA analyst who had put the mission in motion, crying nearby, looking down at the man she spent half a decade searching for. Everyone at Jalalabad spent the next day congratulating each other and posing for pictures before another forty-five-minute flight, this time back to Bagram.

After chicken fingers, French fries, and coffee, Bisonette and the other SEALs stowed their gear, then began the debriefing at tables designated for each room in the three-story house harboring bin Laden. While someone drew a diagram of the compound and floor plans for the main structure and guesthouse, Bisonette watched a photographic specialist download the contents of his digital camera into a computer; seconds later, he stared at the images he had taken. When one of the SEALs apologized for the boxes left behind, a CIA analyst told them that the materials seized might take months to go through. Two hours later, the SEALs watched Rangers carry bin Laden's body away to be eventually buried at sea after an Islamic service.

THE SECOND KILLING

Almost five years later, controversial journalist and investigative reporter Seymour M. Hersh claimed in his book *The Killing of Osama bin Laden* that Pakistan's two leading generals may have known about the mission in advance. Hersh concluded after extensive but largely anonymous interviews that bin Laden may have been held at Abbottabad for at least five years. Hersh reported that certain Pakistani officials had received advance notice of the raid and arranged for the Americans to cross Pakistan airspace. Finally, Hersh contends that bin Laden's whereabouts were disclosed by a former Pakistani intelligence official rather than through American efforts tracking a bin Laden courier. The Pakistani informant may have received some $20 million or more in reward money, according to Hersh.

The Hersh version of events relates that an informant walked into the U.S. embassy in Islamabad in August 2010 met with initial skepticism by the CIA but passed a polygraph test. The compound that the informant identified was put under surveillance, according to one anonymous informant Hersh relies on. After the informant left Afghanistan with his family to become a CIA consultant, intelligence and military officials in Washington began discussing their options in this version of events.

Two months later, after an initial briefing, President Obama directed the intelligence operators to get proof of identity before coming back to the White House. American intelligence now turned to Pakistan.

Decades-old public feuding between the Pakistani and U.S. intelligence communities provided good cover for ongoing back-channel exchanges of information. The Pakistanis provided information about the Taliban, whom the Pakistanis viewed as a potential source of troops if war with India ever erupted. The bin Laden compound was less than a fifteen-minute helicopter ride away from the Pakistan Army Aviation air base at Tarbela Garzi. This base became an important covert operations center for the Pakistan Inter-Service Intelligence agency only three miles from a Pakistani combat battalion headquarters.

In early January, a physician who sometimes treated bin Laden provided DNA proof, in exchange for reward money, that the terrorist was indeed living in Abbottabad. An American team consisting of a SEAL, a CIA officer, and two communications specialists set up a liaison office at Tarbela Garzi, according to the Hersh sources, even as, according to Hersh, under-the-table American cash payments to Pakistani officials began to dry up.

While versions of events and analysis of American and Pakistani motives differ, the sources interviewed by Hersh agree that the two countries negotiated a deal. The American cash spigot would be turned on again in exchange for American access to bin Laden. F-16 airplanes that had been ordered would be delivered. This alternative Hersh story relates that the SEAL and the CIA operators at Tarbela Garzi would coordinate the SEAL-led operation with senior U.S. officers in Afghanistan.

According to Hersh, American authorities had originally planned to delay any announcement about the killing of bin Laden for seven days and withhold details of the Pakistani cooperation permanently.

Operational details provided by Hersh also varied from versions told by others. Hersh relates that the Pakistan Inter-Service Intelligence operators guarding bin Laden abandoned him when they heard the American helicopters. Several SEALs blew their way through steel doors on the first and second floors of the bin Laden house. Then they went through the second door on the right on the third floor and shot bin Laden where he stood, unarmed though he was. Hersh contends that the SEALs stuffed some books and papers found in bin Laden's bedroom into bags but didn't take any computers or computer data devices.

The Hersh sources also disputed the version of events as related by the White House and other sources describing the bin Laden house in Abbottabad as a center for al-Qaeda operations. Despite alleged assurances to the Pakistanis that the death of bin Laden would not be made public for seven days, President Obama reported it to the nation within hours because the destruction of the Black Hawk inside the compound made earlier disclosure through Pentagon leaks inevitable. Secretary of State Clinton was the lone high-level dissenter, according to Hersh, insisting that the seven-day information embargo promised to the Pakistanis should be kept.

Hersh sources also disputed Bisonette's version of events, claiming that during their first debriefing after the mission, Bisonette and another SEAL identified as Rob O'Neill made no mention of any opposition at all when they entered the bin Laden residence. Hersh also claimed in his book that material provided to the Pentagon press corps five days after the raid portraying bin Laden watching himself on television was a fabrication. Hersh also questioned claims that bin Laden was directing an al-Qaeda command-and-control center at the time of his death. These dissenting sources, according to Hersh, also claimed that Dr. Aziz, the physician who occasionally treated bin Laden, obtained protection from Pakistani retribution by naming another Pakistani doctor, Shakil Afridi, as the source of the bin Laden DNA sample.

Finally, according to these dissenting voices, bin Laden's burial at sea conducted on USS *Carl Vinson* never happened. Hersh reported in *The Killing of Osama Bin Laden* that according to one source, the CIA took bin Laden's body to Afghanistan, while yet another source reported that Americans threw bin Laden's remains off the helicopter over the Hindu Kush mountain range during the return flight to Jalalabad.

THE THIRD KILLING

Scott Kerr, a member of SEAL Team Six, got word that something important was going on one January morning in Virginia Beach when the JSOC chief of staff ordered him to fly into the JSOC headquarters by 3:00 that afternoon for a meeting with Admiral William McRaven and a CIA operator on an unspecified mission. Kerr had made this trip so often by then that he even kept a special briefcase filled with paperwork for the chopper flight.

The meeting in the dingy gray underground conference room at JSOC, a stone's throw from the admiral's office, included Kerr, McRaven, and a CIA counterterrorism expert named "Walter Youngblood." They sat with thick gray folders that remained closed on a conference table until a guard closed the door and activated a sign in the hallway indicating that a meeting was in progress. "We're going to need some of your guys for some planning," McRaven told Kerr and the others. An unspecified high-target individual required immediate action. Kerr knew this could be bin Laden. Still, other targets might have prompted the CIA to request yet another "Pet SEAL" operation, in which SEALs did all the heavy lifting. The SEALs had recently conducted a September 2008 mission into Waziristan, far to the north of Kabul, only to find nothing.

Given that a $25 million reward dangled over bin Laden's head for years, many intelligence operators assumed him dead or under the protection of a friendly government. One "boogeyman" theory held that Pakistani intelligence had killed him but kept him "alive" to keep American money flowing into their bank accounts. Yet another variant theory supposed that bin Laden was still alive but gripped in a leadership struggle with upstart Ayman Zawahiri.

After some prompting, Walter began telling Kerr what the CIA knew so far. The one-and-a-half-acre target compound had no telephone lines and no internet service. At least half of the two dozen people inside were children. The armed security, if any, was invisible, but at least five armed military-age men lived inside. A three-sided box on top of the building might hold Strela helicopter-killing missiles, but that was unconfirmed. Kerr asked whether the CIA thought the target was Bert or Ernie, the SEALs' pet names for bin Laden and Zawahiri. Walter didn't get the joke since the CIA called bin Laden "Crankshaft" but intimated that the target was well over six feet tall. CIA voice print analysts expressed a 60 to 70 percent level of confidence identifying the target as bin Laden. During a meeting scheduled for March 14, Walter planned to tell President Obama that the operational options included a smart bomb, a combined operation with a host nation deemed hostile, or a unilateral American action; the three men spent the next few minutes discussing the third option.

Now Kerr wondered whether the target lived in Lebanon, Iran, Syria, or maybe even Libya or Somalia. Keeping these questions to himself, he moved on to the operational details, narrowing the possibilities along the way. Walter revealed that the round-trip helicopter distance was 200 miles and paused. During the silence, Kerr pondered the difficulties of refueling helicopters before Admiral McRaven told him that the helicopters would be Ghost Hawks, choppers so quiet and highly classified that usually only SEAL Team Six and Delta Force rode in them. These "Jedi Rides" supposedly awaited use in locked, guarded hangars. The Jedi were flown only at night on only the most important missions, invisible to radar.

Now McRaven directed Kerr to recall a SEAL squadron currently on stand-down going through training school. The training and planning for the VIP mission would be ninety days. The squadron leadership would office at CIA headquarters in Langley, Virginia. McRaven and Youngblood each pushed a gray folder across the table. On the way out, Kerr passed a Ghost Hawk helicopter squadron commander he once worked with, knowing full well that Colonel Jim Overall would now receive the same briefing Kerr had just been through with one important addition. Within a few minutes, Overall would know exactly where they would be going.

Kerr thought through the possibility that, this time, the SEALs might take out bin Laden or become the fall guys if something went wrong. This might depend on the "commander's intent," ideally a clear one-sentence description of the mission objective. In practice, however, that sentence might direct that the target be "interdicted" (killed) or "neutralized," which might not include lethal force. Kerr's orders, when received, stated that the target was to be interdicted. And the target described in those orders was nonpermissive, meaning that the operation would be conducted in a country that the United States considered hostile.

On Sunday, May 1, 2011, as darkness fell in Jalalabad, four-star Admiral William (Bill) McRaven needed some fresh air after twelve hours of debriefings while communications experts continued setting up the computer hardware, cables, and paraphernalia enabling real-time connections between the White House, the Pentagon, and CIA operators. Abandoned Soviet helicopters and gunships from the days when Jalalabad served as a Soviet air base twenty-three years earlier littered the ground around him. Since Taliban insurgents had attacked the air base five months earlier in late 2010, two heavily armed SEALs stayed with Admiral McRaven at all times. Among the stars now emerging in the darkness above Jalalabad, four reconnaissance satellites photographed the ground below, facilitating communications, and reporting the weather. The KH-12 Keyhole snapped high-resolution images of a lone figure walking in a garden behind twenty-foot walls just outside Abbottabad. McRaven now watched an RQ-170 Sentinel drone, "the Beast of Kandahar," quickly roll down the runway and take off, leaving nothing in its wake.

Along the path back to the command center, McRaven no doubt wondered again whether he was sending these SEALs into a trap. Even though 9/11 was now very old news, there was every reason to wonder why following bin Laden's courier right into the compound was so easy. Clearly, Zawahari had every reason to set bin Laden up and become the odds-on favorite to lead al-Qaeda. He knew that machine guns hidden on the third floor of bin Laden's lair or even SA-7 Soviet SAMs fired from launchers no larger than bazookas could take out the American helicopters, giving these al-Qaeda sickos something to celebrate just in time for the tenth anniversary of 9/11. McRaven delayed going back into the operations center for a minute or two, knowing that his men needed time to finish planning without worrying about an admiral listening in.

McRaven became a political player less than a month earlier, on the first Wednesday in April, when President Obama promoted him to four-star admiral and appointed him the first SEAL to lead JSOC. Now, as the Beast of Kandahar soared high above Abbottabad and began sending video in real time to his command center, Admiral McRaven began to feel increasingly confident about the mission ahead.

Others at the White House 11,000 miles away didn't share this degree of confidence since they might be on the front lines politically if anything went wrong tonight. Plans for air support for the helicopters died due to a perfectly rational fear that the fighters might make this a larger, more visible operation, increasing the possibility of a confrontation with the Pakistani air forces. Originally, the latest Black Hawk helicopters, called Ghost Hawks, with the very best avionics and electronics available, were designated to fly the mission. Now that the fighter support from USS *Carl Vinson* was gone, the planners pulled the new Ghost Hawks out of the mission for fear that if they were shot down for lack of fighter support, highly sensitive and secret new technology could be compromised. And that in turn meant that a refueling point somewhere between Abbottabad and Jalalabad would be needed.

An accident at such a refueling position doomed the 1979 mission to rescue American hostages held in Iran. Despite the passage of thirty-two years, the refueling operation in Afghanistan would be very similar to the one attempted during the ill-fated Operation Eagle Claw. This time, two CH-47 helicopters would meet the SEALs at a dry riverbed just inside Afghanistan. Flashlight 1 carried fuel bladders, hoses, and other gear; the second helicopter would carry twenty SEAL Team Six operators to guard the four American helicopters from Taliban insurgents. The SEALs carried stinger antiaircraft missiles, anticipating the possibility that Pakistani fighters would chase the Black Hawks over the border. An EA-6B Prowler electronic warfare plane was added to the operation at the last minute to jam Pakistani air defenses during the time the SEALs operated in Pakistan. The live feed at 9:00 p.m. on Sunday, May 1, from the Beast of Kandahar drone flying above the bin Laden compound on the edge of Abbottabad was so granular that it displayed a bodyguard checking the lock on the front gate from 20,000 feet above.

The two stealth Hawks would each carry ten SEAL assaulters, including snipers and two demolition experts. Razor 2 also carried a designated spotter to direct fire into the doors and windows of the target building as necessary. The plan called for the first stealth Hawk, Razor 1, to land on the roof of the main house and work toward the ground. Razor 2 would provide sniper cover from the air until Razor 2 operators blazed into the building. The second helicopter would land on the guest-house roof, from which the second team would descend to the ground floor, cross the compound grounds to the front door of the main house, and neutralize any shooters, ideally within thirty seconds. Two Chinook CH-47 helicopters, one carrying the command team and the second equipped with Gatling guns, would hover above to provide covering fire. At the last minute, a Pakistani-American CIA case officer joined the team after a quick lesson in fast-rope assaults. Intelligence suggested as many as eight military-age armed men among the two dozen or more people in the compound with bin Laden. The second stealth Hawk carried an explosive-sniffing dog named Karo.

Back in Washington at 2:00 that afternoon (9:00 p.m. Afghanistan/Pakistan time), Vice President Biden, Secretary of Defense Gates, and Secretary of State Clinton gathered at the White House in a conference room. CIA Director Leon Panetta, assisted by an experienced SEAL team operator, provided commentary by video link. In Afghanistan, the operation launched at 10:00 p.m. local time, with the two stealth Hawks leading the command helicopter and two helicopters assigned to do the fueling toward Abbottabad some 208 miles to the east. They arrived on target on time at 12:59 a.m. local time. The snipers aboard Razor 2, hovering above the guesthouse, noticed a man come out of the guesthouse carrying an AK-47 that he lifted and fired to his left. Within seconds, the snipers aboard Razor 2 killed Ahmed Al-Kuwaitee as well as Kuwaitee's wife standing immediately behind him.

The stealth Hawks are so quiet that Kuwaitee likely did not hear the choppers until just before they arrived. On the third floor of the main house, a seven-foot wall providing privacy for a patio outside sliding glass doors probably blocked the first helicopter noises. Soon, the down blast of Razor 2 knocked plastic porch chairs against the windows of bin Laden's bedroom as it landed on the roof just above the bin Laden terrace. Several of the SEALs came through terrace glass doors leading into the hallway next to bin Laden's bedroom just as bin Laden stuck his head out into the hallway and slammed the door. Bin Laden's son, Khalid bin Laden, quickly took two bullets as he ran up the stairs toward his father's room. And once the SEALs burst into the bin Laden bedroom, they saw an AKSU machine gun leaning against his bed in a room later described as scented like old clothing.

Four SEAL bullets quickly sought the target. Two struck home, the last one piercing bin Laden's skull, killing him immediately. Soon, the second stealth Hawk lowered itself onto the guesthouse roof to deal with the occupants there just as they heard someone on the radio reporting bin Laden's location on the third floor of the main house. Razor 2 SEALs, in the meantime, began clearing every room in the guesthouse one by one, stepping over Kuwaitee, the courier they had killed from the air minutes earlier just after 1:00 a.m. The Chinook helicopters in the distance became audible just as the SEALs assigned to the guesthouse began searching for missiles that might bring them down and strand them all in Abbottabad.

Kerr, the mission commander, arrived just in time to join the guesthouse SEALs hurrying through what was left of the front gate, past a barn full of chickens and a pair of water buffalo. After blowing a hole through the wall surrounding the main house, a dozen SEALs or more spread out over the first floor while Arshad Khan waited in the darkness with an AK-47 two seconds too long. From his hiding spot in a bedroom, Kerr made his way to the third floor, past bin Laden's dead son Khalid, and toward the bedroom. The dead body on the floor became visible in Washington, D.C., and elsewhere thanks to the satellites above, even as the SEALs drew DNA samples. One of the team members held up bin Laden's loaded AK-47, saying that a 9-mm pistol was also found. Kerr radioed Washington and reported "Apache, OK," meaning that none of the SEALs or their teammates sustained wounds, before confirming that Al-Kuwuiti, Arshad Khan, and Khalid bin Laden were dead. Bin Laden's son Hamza, thought to be in the compound, remained free. Kerr kept the most important killed-in-action code for the last: Geronimo. Eleven thousand miles away, President Obama summed it all up in three words: "We got him."

According to one source, a photograph of Secretary Clinton, Vice President Biden, and President Obama, often identified with the very moment they learned that bin Laden was dead, in fact records their reaction on seeing one of the stealth Hawks crash moments later. Chuck Pfarrer wrote in *SEAL Target Geronimo* that Razor 1, the second stealth Hawk on the scene, now lifted from the roof of the main residence and flew briefly toward a landing zone on the road a football field west of the command Chinook but began to drop toward the ground due to a flight deck control failure. The "green unit" that controlled computer inputs and outputs was down; according to this version of events, the computer failure caused the stealth Hawk to sink tail first into the compound as the sniper crew aboard Razor 2 watched dust rise in the air from the animal pen below.

Pfarrer writes that two operators heard the noise from the crash as they carried bin Laden's body out of the main house into the compound grounds just as someone on the ground reported that Razor 1 was down, twenty minutes into the operation. Despite the crash, the teams on-site continued the mission, loading bin Laden's body and at least a dozen garbage bags filled with actionable intelligence. Kerr told everyone they would be leaving in ten minutes as he assessed the stealth Hawk wreckage, now being scavenged by the crew. The SEALs and their team blew up everything of any possible help to the Taliban, including the avionics and flight deck and other controls. Later, Pfarrer reported that the noncombatants at the compound were questioned and photographed. At least one of the women received a tetanus shot as team members took extensive, detailed photographs of the terrorists, the rooms they died in, clothing, ammunition found, and even the bed where bin Laden slept.

Of equal importance, according to this account some 500 or so notebooks, accounting ledgers, wire diagrams for bombs, hard drives, disk drives, laptops, monitors, and notebook journals written in Arabic and even English were discovered. According to Pfarrer, these documents indicated that bin Laden was planning an attack. Once the remnants of Razor 1 were wired with explosives on a three-minute timer, Kerr and his command team lifted into the air to watch the fireworks.

In the weeks to come, following President Obama's 11:30 p.m. announcement on Sunday, May 1, the world learned that the SEALs and the CIA had spearheaded the operation, though many divergent stories of the details circulated in Washington and elsewhere.

According to Pfarrer, a dozen bullets fired by SEAL Team Six operators killed bin Laden, two bodyguards, and one of his sons, all of whom carried weapons or had loaded weapons within their reach.

Initial cooperation between the CIA Office of Public Affairs and journalists and screenwriters ended after the White House sent out word during the week of June 8 that anyone leaking information about the Abbottabad raid would be fired. SEALs participating in the raid now criticized the public disclosures, arguing that al-Qaeda should have been kept in the dark until the rest of its leadership cadre could be neutralized. Worse yet, according to these sources, al-Qaeda now knew the extent to which computers and hard drives at Chateau Osama were compromised, even as some elements of the press publicized the locations of SEAL family neighborhoods during live TV broadcasts. In the months to come, an article in a national magazine portrayed the Abbottabad mission as something akin to an organized crime battle amidst speculation that Sony Pictures might be given possibly inappropriate access to classified information for a project that eventually became the film *Zero Dark Thirty*.

Despite the various versions of these events, one thing is certain. President Obama and Vice President Biden met a number of the SEALs, pilots, CIA operators, and others involved in the Abbottabad raid during a ceremony at Fort Campbell, Kentucky, five days later on Friday, May 6. He asked the Razor 1 team which of them killed Osama and was told that everyone on the mission deserved the credit.

So say us all.

CHAPTER SIXTEEN

The Folded Flag

Eight years after beginning her career in Cincinnati, Jessica Buchanan became an education adviser to the Danish Demining Group, an NGO operating in Somalia. Jessica worked in Hargeisa, as well as in the Demining Group field office 600 miles to the southeast, in Galkayo, on the very edge of a region controlled by Al Shabab, an Islamist group that ruled through terror tactics and Sharia law.

Her road to Galkayo was hardly conventional. After becoming a teacher in the Philadelphia area, she began volunteering for NGOs during summer school vacations, first in Honduras but later in South Sudan, Uganda, Kenya, and Rwanda. She first traveled to Hargeisa, a city of some 1.5 million souls in northern Somalia, a few years earlier to develop classroom material for the local population on how to avoid the advanced war munitions and land mines then creating a generation of young amputees.

Jessica and a fellow worker from Denmark, Poul Thisted, returned to Galkayo on Monday, October 24, 2011, despite worsening conditions there. Jessica's husband of two years, Erik Landemalm, a veteran of the Swedish navy's Special Operation Forces and now working as an NGO project manager, was very concerned about the possible dangers she faced on this trip. She knew the dangers but couldn't put it off a third time. Jessica was going south of the "Green Line" running through Galkayo, the very real yet officially invisible border between areas controlled by the Somalian government and the territories partially controlled by Al Shabab.

Jessica jumped off the UN flight with several bags stuffed with computers and training materials. She texted Erik joking that he should come get her if she and Poul were kidnapped. During an earlier trip to this satellite office in South Galkayo, Jessica listened to gunfire on a nearby street while conducting her classroom lesson on avoiding land mines. Some Somalians despised westerners such as Jessica and Poul, seeing them as infidel ransom bait at best.

The local NGO security manager and a driver they didn't know picked up Poul and Jessica after their flight, dropped them at the NGO guesthouse just north of the Green Line, and picked them up the next morning. Today, Jessica and Poul worked with no gunfire in the background before loading their gear for the twenty-minute trip back to the safety on the north side of the Green Line in the NGO Land Cruiser.

Ten minutes later, their lives changed. Men in Somali Special Protection Unit uniforms surrounded the Land Cruiser, pointing AK-47s at Jessica and Poul. They opened the doors, grabbed Abdiriza (the local NGO security manager), and went through the motions of beating him up without inflicting any serious damage. Jessica noticed that Abdiriza didn't look the least bit surprised when the "new" NGO driver whom Jessica never saw before drove away at the command of "Ali," the lead kidnapper. Ali was an acne-faced thirty-something six-footer with the frantic eyes of someone who just chewed more than a little khat, a plant that has the effect of amphetamines. Ali started the conversation by pointing his old AK-47 at Jessica's head and screaming the word "mobile" until everyone in the Land Cruiser handed Ali their cell phones.

Minutes later, as they bumped up and down through bad backcountry roads, Jessica began hoping that this was a robbery. That happened to many westerners in Kenya taken into the countryside, robbed of their money and car keys, but allowed to escape alive. Poul, who carried no such illusions, simply whispered the one thing Jessica didn't want to hear: this was abduction.

Now Jessica began to notice that Ali was not the only one hopped up on khat. The other two abductors began yelling for Poul to shut up as Jessica began regretting her text to Erik about being kidnapped on this trip. Worse still, Ali began taking their jewelry, prompting Jessica to hide hers in the trip bag that Ali would eventually search. Now Jessica thought back to her Hostile Environment Individual Safety Training (HEIST), in which the instructors emphasized the importance of not showing anger or any other emotion. Students in the training group, including Jessica and Poul, had learned to memorize the phone number of at least one potential ransom source, as if their lives depended on it. The unspoken problem in this region was religious. Abduction by any ideologue bent on making a statement meant certain death, often in a public execution. On the other hand, Jessica remembered, survival beyond the first twenty-four hours often dramatically increased the chances of coming out alive.

During the next few hours, the abductors changed cars several times, adding a young boy about eight years old to their crew during the third stop. The junior abductor was dressed like the others: turban headed with a loose shirt over baggy trousers. All carried heavy ammunition belts, indicating sophisticated planning by pirates or Al Shabab rather than a random kidnapping. Late that night, the convoy ground to a halt on the edge of some scrub brush. Ali, the abduction leader, now ordered Jessica and Poul to begin walking before he disappeared. Later, under a moonless, starlit sky, the eight-year-old pointed his AK-47 at Jessica and began laughing in a way that confirmed what Jessica already suspected: he too was high on khat leaves, wild-eyed and eager for an excuse to shoot her. Jessica noticed that some of the men carried long-bladed knives. She wondered if she and Poul were going to be beheaded when ordered onto their knees. Poul and Jessica turned their backs on the kidnappers.

Within hours, President Obama and the FBI knew about the kidnapping as well as the long odds for a successful rescue mission. Jessica's husband, Erik, and her father, John Buchanan, had learned about the abduction before the FBI but contacted no one for fear that publicity might cause the kidnappers to panic. Within minutes, an FBI agent in Nairobi called Erik and assured him that the agency was now searching for Jessica and Poul. In those early days, there was no actionable intelligence to act on, although Al Shabab was suspected from the beginning.

Back in Somalia, Poul and Jessica learned late on the evening of October 25 that they would not be executed after all. The kidnappers marched them to a new location in the desert early the next morning, even as the authorities in Washington most certainly decided that once the two NGO workers showed up, the DEVGRU SEALs of SEAL Team Six would be sent to rescue them. Poul and Jessica were worth money, big money, or so the abduction chairman thought, whoever he was. Day 3 brought some certainty about their routine, at least for the present. During the day, the kidnap party of about twenty-two, including the captives, rested under acacia trees. During the nights that followed under the open desert skies, hostages and kidnappers stayed at "the Banda place," an open shelter with a thatched roof. While there, Jessica and Poul slept in an open goat pen.

Soon, a forty-something kidnap leader named Abdi introduced himself to Jessica. He was something of a chatterbox, as long as the khat leaves held out, talking about his philosophy and asking Jessica questions Abdi didn't really expect the American to answer. Abdi ordered in khat leaves, cigarettes, and Coca-Cola. Jessica came to believe that Abdi considered abducting these two Americans to be payback of sorts for his years of poverty. Abdi reminded Jessica that every dog has his day. She hoped that Abdi's day was coming soon.

Two days later, she noticed that the eight-year-old boy who had pointed an AK-47 at her wore one of the bracelets her NGO handed out to kids who attended classes on avoiding war munitions and land mines. Jessica and Poul talked briefly just before Abdi's replacement arrived. Jabriel was older than the others, described himself as a translator from Mogadishu, and told the captives that their ransom price was $45 million. Jabriel snorted that the pirates (his term) might be lucky to get $1 million for Jessica and Poul. Later, on day 5, October 29, the pirates drove Jessica into the desert for her "proof-of-life" call, but neither her husband nor her father could talk because their phones didn't work. But no worry, as Jabriel gave her a third number to call. Mohammed, the voice on the end of the line, identified himself as an assistant to the regional security manager in the Danish NGO that Jessica and Poul worked for. Jessica answered questions about her first dog and other personal proof-of-life questions, hoping that her family might soon know that she was alive. Jessica watched Abdi and her new best friend, Jabriel, argue about how much ransom she and Poul should bring in the next day. After Abdi threw a sucker punch, Jabriel limped over to the captives and told them that the ransom demand was $18 million. The Americans begged him to stay, and Jabriel agreed to do just that. Weeks later, Jabriel told Poul and Jessica that there was talk among the pirates of selling them to Al Shabab since the pirates weren't getting anywhere in the negotiations. Eventually, Abdi, the pirate captain, became so frustrated with the lack of progress that he knocked Poul down and threatened to send two American heads to Mohammed, the Danish NGO negotiator.

While negotiations between the NGO and the pirates ground on, Jessica's husband Erik learned that although the U.S. government knew the exact location where she and Poul languished, the chances of successfully rescuing them from the drug-fueled pirates alive were not good. Such a rescue attempt, Erik was told, would not be launched as long as negotiations continued, unless Jessica or Poul faced immediate danger or failing health.

The crisis management team, consisting of selected Danish NGO managers, professional hostage negotiators, and the FBI, eventually learned that the pirates received daily shipments from Adado (also called Caadado), a city of 49,000 in central Somalia. The Americans planning a possible rescue operation knew that local Somalian authorities could not be trusted.

Old Jabriel now began making physical advances to Jessica while sniffing that the NGO's last offer for the hostages was $300,000. Finally, several pirate "journalists" filmed Poul and Jessica reading pleas for payment of the ransom demands. "We know you have more money than this," Jessica begged, ridiculing the latest NGO offer before imploring NGO negotiators to get serious. Abdi then told the Americans they must close the deal in one week.

Although that week passed without any consequences, the pirates changed their negotiation tactics. Abdi began pressuring Poul and Jessica to call the Danish Refugee Council. Jessica was eventually allowed to speak with Erik, her husband, but the negotiations went nowhere. Worse still, Jabriel, the friendly but stooped older man, became increasingly aggressive toward Jessica. Weeks into the kidnapping, Poul and Jessica had met a real pirate, one Captain Bashir, a thirty-five-year-old Chubster with dark skin, bad acne, and a silver Land Cruiser. After a particularly frustrating session with a new NGO negotiator named Lisa, Bashir pointed his AK-47 at Poul and led him away.

Moments later, Jessica sobbed to the NGO negotiator that Poul was gone. Something must be done soon. Nearly 8,000 miles away in Washington, Jessica's husband, Erik, demanded to know what the FBI was going to do. Abdi, the on-scene pirate crew leader, had disappeared two days after Christmas as Jessica watched lights blink in the distance. No one from "the International City," as Abado, Somalia, described itself, was coming to the rescue of the Americans. Worse, the kidnappers often displayed Jessica and Poul there as if their abduction were an open secret.

Shortly after Abdi left, the eight-year-old khat addict whom Jessica now called "Crack Baby" returned to the hostage camp with another child-soldier named Hassan, brandishing his AK-47 and pushing Jessica around to show off. A few days later, Poul was returned to the hostage camp—alive despite Jessica's worst fears—just as the abductors began looking at the skies with fear on their faces. New Year's Day 2012 came and went without any fanfare—just another day in the Somalian desert. Twenty-four days later, a week and a day after yet another routine proof-of-life call, Jessica suffered once again from the same urinary tract infection that had plagued her almost from the beginning of this ordeal. Despite this illness, she cooked the meat from a live goat brought into camp to treat the kidnappers that Tuesday.

Jessica was a vegetarian but shared in the feast anyway. As the sun went down, Jessica treated herself to a vision of being home with Erik, holding their first baby. The Nairobi FBI office began working the case when the abduction was reported. Contrary to popular belief, the FBI rather than the CIA was and is responsible for investigating crimes against American citizens committed in foreign countries. Ninety-three days into the FBI rescue operation, the American government identified the kidnappers as all but certainly a consortium of three southern Somalian subclans of the Habr Gidir. The Nairobi FBI office, about 700 miles southwest of Mogadishu, knew that some twenty-six men and teenage boys served as guards in the kidnap camp. Human intelligence sources disclosed that medicine forwarded to treat Jessica's thyroid condition was never dispensed; she was being killed in slow motion by a urinary tract infection accelerated by filthy, primitive conditions. This was the trip wire that brought in the SEALs thanks to Erik's constant calls.

On January 23, the day before Jessica prepared the goat feast near Adado, Somalia, President Obama got the bad news from his team: the negotiations and the health of the two hostages were failing even as a rescue opportunity approached. The initial rescue planning began that very day.

Djibouti, the capital of the country of the same name, hosts Camp Lemonier, the only permanent American air base in Africa, home of the Command Joint Task Force–Horn of Africa, some 1,200 miles north of Mogadishu. And it was there that the SEAL operation began.

Twenty-four SEALs jumped out of the plane from an altitude of 27,000 feet, free-falling into the pitch-black, cool darkness of an early Wednesday morning, landing in scrub brush near some low-slung buildings. Each SEAL wore a vest weighing sixty pounds, providing solid protection against AK-47 fire but hardly any guarantee of safety at all if the abductors targeted them with grenade launchers or heavy machine gun fire. Each SEAL wore desert camouflage but, more important, the latest in night-vision equipment, providing four infrared vision tubes for a wider, sharper view and maximum depth perception. This time, on this mission, no pirate would be taken alive; they would be killed as quickly as possible when encountered for fear that a surviving pirate would kill the two hostages without hesitation.

One important element in the local culture was greatly to the SEALs' advantage. Islam considered dogs unclean; even unreligious people in this region didn't keep pets because of the endemic poverty here. Thus, they need not worry about barking dogs.

The SEALs carried light weapons on this mission: Heckler & Koch MP-7 machine pistols as well as the H & K 416 assault rifles and long-bladed knives, the American weapons of choice. The SEALs silently closed in on the kidnap camp knowing where Erik and Jessica usually slept. Typically, the kidnappers lit campfires but not this morning. All the guards slept as Jessica walked around the camp—and that was a problem.

Later, Jessica recalled waking up at about 2:00 local time the morning of January 25 on a moonless night looking at stars barely visible behind a heavy haze. The urinary tract infection might just cost her another night's sleep. This might be problem enough at home, but here, going to the toilet could easily get somebody shot. She called out a brief warning that she was getting up (not that anyone was listening). The pirates still slept—or so it seemed. Poul and Jessica typically slept surrounded by nine guards with twenty feet between the two groups, yet no one else appeared to be awake.

Jessica yelled out "toilet" once more, once again meeting only silence, then shrugged and picked up a small penlight that was barely working. A few yards away behind a bush, she fantasized about quietly creeping over to Poul, waking him up, and vanishing into the darkness. Maybe, just maybe, they could escape. There might be enough water along the eighty-four-mile escape route she dreamed about to keep them alive but probably not—and so, with that dismal thought, she returned to what passed as her bed.

Through the past ninety-three nights outside, Jessica had become accustomed to animal noises, insects buzzing, and the occasional snap of a single twig in the darkness. Yet what she now heard, gradually becoming louder, struck her as something different. Curious, she stood up on her sleeping mat, pointing a penlight here and there among the pirates and their gear. She had begun to reconsider the dim prospects of escaping this place alive when new noises, these closer than before, jolted her senses. This time she wasn't alone. Dahir, the closest thing to her friend among these pirates, stood up and began whispering the word "African" as he cocked a rifle. The second time he whispered the code word, Jessica could hear pirates all around her cocking weapons before the gunfire erupted.

Was this another clan coming to steal the two hostages or, worse yet, Al Shabab? Either way, she soon heard the thud of bullets into flesh, screams, death rattles, and Dahir whispering "Oh, no" before a brief silence. Now someone said "Jessica" in an American voice. "We've come to take you home," the SEAL said, but the gunfire in the darkness continued, more slowly, as a man she did not know threw her on his back. The rescuer took her to a nearby clearing. A SEAL returned to Jessica's sleeping mat three times for her belongings while she wondered what had happened to Poul, finally asking about him. An arm extended out to her in the darkness—it was him. After a minute of idle chatter, Poul and Jessica, now wearing her shoes, began following the SEALs at a slow run toward some helicopters. Jessica dove into the first one she saw as Poul piled in behind her. Men in helmets, face masks, and goggles—heroes who might be mistaken for space aliens surrounded them. She had lived to tell her story in the memoir *Impossible Odds*, written with her husband, Erik Landemalm, and Anthony Flacco.

These American heroes surrounding her now were all SEALs—and one of the SEALs handed Jessica a neatly folded American flag.

CHAPTER SEVENTEEN

We're All Going to Die

"IF YOU DON'T GET HERE SOON, WE'RE ALL GOING TO DIE," SAID THE caller on September 11, 2012; he was in the American consulate at Benghazi, Libya, requesting urgent action from CIA security officers at their annex less than a mile away. Several of the CIA operators, including Jack Silva (not his real name), were retired as Navy SEALs. Silva arrived at Benghazi the previous month to join the Global Response Staff (GRS) comprised of CIA officers and contract special operators. The GRS numbers included many alumni of the SEALs, Green Berets, and Army Rangers.

Silva arrived on a Turkish airliner, cautious of his surroundings from the very beginning of this new lucrative job. The terminal building smelled of flies, body odor, and things unmentionable. From time to time, others crowding the luggage carousel shot him hostile stares, sensing that he was an American. He followed one of the men he had noticed earlier through the doors to a filthy Toyota that was once white. Inside the cab, Silva greeted his SEAL buddy Tyrone "Rone" Woods, who drove them toward a rented property that served as the CIA annex.

Silva and Woods signed on to guard spies, diplomats, and anyone else working out of the U.S. Special Mission Compound (called the Diplomatic Compound) less than a mile from the annex. During the drive, Woods described Benghazi as a lawless place where no one could be relied on but other Americans. Benghazi was Libya's second city, a Chicago of sorts, with a population exceeding 700,000 living in brown, dusty streets within sight of the clear, blue Mediterranean, which brought the Greeks there around 630 BCE, 440 miles from a Roman settlement near present-day Tripoli.

Libya, conquered by the Ottoman Empire in 1511 CE, was little more than a worthless desert until established as an independent monarchy with its own king after World War II. Eight years later, in 1959, the poorest country in the world became an overnight oasis with the discovery of enough oil to export a million barrels a day. Muammar Gaddafi, a young army officer, overthrew King Idris in a 1969 bloodless coup. A revolt against Gaddafi that began in Benghazi forty-two years later resulted in his removal from power—with extreme prejudice—on October 20, 2011, ten months before Jack Silva arrived in Benghazi.

Silva grew up in northern California, attended private high school, but after one day at a university decided to join the Navy and eventually become a SEAL. After basic training and one failed effort to attend BUD/S, he became an airman aboard an aircraft carrier. Later, he passed the BUD/S test and began a decade of sensitive missions in Kosovo and some nineteen other countries. When not in the Middle East, he spent his spare time flipping properties in California during periodic visits to his family.

Silva met Tyrone Woods during naval special warfare training at Miland, California, just outside El Centro, some ten years before this Benghazi assignment. Woods was awarded the Bronze Star with "V" (Valor) insignia for service in Iraq before retiring from the SEALs in 2010. Silva and Woods each joined the GRS to work with other former SEALs while getting as much as $150,000 annually to do something exciting—and dangerous. The year before Woods retired, three GRS veterans died at the hands of a suicide bomber in Afghanistan. Yet that December 2009 tragedy didn't keep Silva and Woods or Silva's friend Glen Doherty from signing up as GRS operators.

The rebellion against Gaddafi began on February 17, 2011. Three months later, the *New York Times* told its readers that some rebels in Benghazi had flown American flags next to their own Libyan pennants, one way of thanking the United States for supporting a no-fly zone that grounded Gaddafi's significant air forces at a critical time. Other rebels blamed the Americans for their troubles. These included the "Partisans of Islamic Law" and another faction aligned with al-Qaeda. After Gaddafi was overthrown, guns could be found anywhere, thanks to numerous rebel raids on government armories. Soon, the largest outdoor market in town featured rocket launchers, grenades, assault rifles, and even mortars, accelerating the number of gunshot wounds treated at Benghazi hospitals from less than fifty the previous year to more than 1,700 in 2011.

Four months before Woods picked Silva up at the Benghazi International Airport, a British diplomatic vehicle blundered into a protest and was attacked. Four days later, on April 6, someone threw a bomb into the American Diplomatic Compound, followed by attacks on the UN office in Benghazi and even the Red Cross. June 6, the anniversary of the D-day invasion of World War II, brought an explosion that blew a large hole in the wall surrounding the Diplomatic Compound, compliments of yet another pro–al-Qaeda group retaliating for the death of its commander in a Pakistan drone attack. The very day Silva arrived in Libya, U.S. Ambassador J. Christopher Stevens called Washington asking for more bodyguards, warning that the security conditions there had become increasingly unpredictable and violent. This followed a June 25 report in which Stevens warned that Islamic radicalism seemed to be on the rise, according to local sources who claimed that several government buildings now flew al-Qaeda flags.

This was to be Woods's last job for the GRS, or so Woods said. Even though he was forty-one years old, his second wife had just delivered his third son. That said, Benghazi seemed no more dangerous than other places where Woods and Silva pulled security duty for the GRS. Silva studied the basic layout of Benghazi even before getting on the plane, courtesy of Google Earth. The city, a port adjacent to the Mediterranean, resembled a spiderweb surrounded by five semicircular roads. During the thirteen-mile run from the airport to the Diplomatic Compound, Woods ran a zigzag course to ditch or at least make things harder for anyone following them.

Several minutes after leaving the airport, Silva noticed a cement checkpoint station straddling the highway. Nearby, three young men in militia uniforms relaxed. One leaned against a pickup truck with a heavy machine gun mounted in the open cargo area.

Several weeks earlier, Woods had confronted Islamist militia fighters at a similar checkpoint while he carried a cargo load of supplies from the airport. Woods and the other GRS operator in the truck raised their rifles and bluffed their way through, while the CIA base chief at the Diplomatic Compound tried to decide whether to send help.

This time, Woods knew instinctively, neither he nor Silva faced any danger, so Woods simply held up his credentials and drove off with a wave. Silva immediately noticed that desert dust covered everything and everybody right down to the horses and sheep nudging their noses through garbage for anything that might keep them alive. This city of 700,000 boasted only one sewage treatment plant, which explained the perpetual stench. Packs of wild dogs searched for food as dozens of cars and trucks burned everywhere, contrasting sharply with the green mountains, palm trees, and the white, sandy beaches in the distance.

They stopped first at the CIA annex consisting of several buildings protected by a wall the height of a basketball rim made of brick and concrete—an open secret in Benghazi. The compound, which once belonged to a rich Libyan, included about two acres of land within an almost perfect square and featured four single-story houses. Privacy was hard to come by here, but the food was good. Silva settled in, got to know the other GRS operators, and hoped that this would be a good assignment. Soon he learned that the U.S. ambassador to Libya, J. Christopher Stevens, would be arriving on Monday, September 10, for a five-day visit.

Stevens, a fifty-two-year-old lifelong bachelor from northern California, had picked up an undergraduate degree in history at the University of California, Berkeley. He spent two years with the Peace Corps in Morocco and then became an international trade law attorney in Washington, hoping to eventually become a diplomat. After becoming fluent in Arabic and serving as a Pearson Fellow staffer for the Senate Foreign Relations Committee, Stevens became deputy chief of the U.S. embassy in Tripoli. He established a relationship with Secretary of State

Condoleezza Rice before her September 2008 trip to Libya by correctly predicting that Gaddafi would flirt with her. After President Obama began his first term, Stevens received his first credentials and began establishing a relationship with rebels opposed to Gaddafi.

The Diplomatic Compound, less than a mile away from the CIA annex in the best neighborhood in Benghazi, covered about eight lush acres conveniently located near the Venezia, an upscale restaurant popular with the diplomatic community. Officially, it became the U.S. Diplomatic Compound in Benghazi. Stevens moved there with his retinue in June 2011 and became ambassador the following May. He returned to Benghazi on Monday September 10, 2012, to open an American library in a local school two days later. That night, Stevens would also meet with the mayor and city council at the El Fadeel Hotel. A friendly Libyan militia called the February 17th Martyrs Brigade agreed to provide additional security, even though the militiamen assigned to the Diplomatic Compound were now staging a strike over low wages and long duty hours. The militiamen on duty refused to protect the ambassador, but the El Fadeel Hotel dinner went on without a hitch.

September 11 began quietly at the compound and drifted into evening. Two GRS operators drove to the local offices of the Arabian Gulf Oil Company that evening as advance work for a morning visit scheduled for the ambassador the next day. The silence around the Diplomatic Compound ended at 9:40 that Tuesday evening with explosions and gunfire at the main gate. Some sixty men, wearing black and white, the colors of al-Qaeda—some old, some young, some bearded, others clean shaven—stormed in through the pedestrian entrance.

Private security operators from British-owned Blue Mountain Group Libya and local February 17th militia guards fled to the farthest corners inside the compound, ceding complete control to the invaders. Within minutes, the invaders set fire to barracks and vehicles, then rushed toward Villa C as alarms went off and a recorded voice calmly advised everyone to duck, cover, and get away from windows. Diplomatic Security (DS) agents at Villa C collected their M4 assault rifles, gear, and armor, including a combat shotgun, and then quickly found Ambassador Stevens. The other DS agents hid in the compound's cantina; two others sheltered in the Tactical Operations Center as the invaders roamed at will through the complex, firing at anything and everything.

Jack Silva first heard about the attack on the radio while finishing an e-mail to his wife. He popped in his contact lenses, grabbed his go-bag, and rushed outside, joining six other lightly armed Americans—all that stood between Ambassador Stevens and the hostile mob. The Global Response Team leader briefed Woods, Silva, and the other three security men at the CIA annex on the substantial force they would soon be facing. The GRS leader assured Woods, Silva, and the other three American reinforcements that a large contingent of February 17th militia fighters would join them at the Diplomatic Compound—or so they hoped.

The five men piled into a Mercedes and a BMW and then waited for word to start the operation, hoping to arrive at Stevens's compound quickly enough to take the initiative with satellite and direct air support. That didn't happen. Instead of the reconnaissance drone and AC-130 Spectre gunship that the five-man relief team had asked for, they received assurances that February 17th Libyan militia members would help the Americans carry out this mission. This didn't reassure the team. Several months earlier at the Benghazi airport, in similar circumstances, the February 17th militia had been ineffective in the face of a robbery attempt that Woods thwarted himself.

While Silva, Woods, and the rest of the relief team cooled their heels, rescuers debated the details of their rescue mission in Benghazi, Tripoli, and Washington. During the wait, former Army Ranger Kris "Tanto" Paronto recruited "Henry," a sixty-something Libyan working as a translator, to go with them even though he did not have a military background. Henry agreed to go and jumped into the Mercedes as orange flames began rising high into the air from the Diplomatic Compound less than a mile away.

The rescue team heard one of the DS agents in the compound with Ambassador Stevens report that as many as thirty men fired at them. The DS agent begged for help but heard only silence on the radio as Ambassador Stevens listened to the intruders blow out the outside front doors with an RPG. DS agent Scott Wickland watched from a hiding place as several men ransacked the villa's living room.

Next, the mob spotted the interior villa entrance to the "safe haven"—several bedrooms with locked metal grilles on the exterior windows. The interior safe-haven entrance consisted of exterior wooden doors hardened with metal. The safe haven included a closet containing water and medical supplies where the ambassador could hide if all else failed.

Wickland quietly warned Ambassador Stevens and Sean Smith, a State Department communications officer, to brace for a grenade attack. After all, that's how the intruders got into the villa. Instead, the attackers carried in cans of diesel fuel found outside near a generator, soaked everything inside the villa, and started a fire, taking the Americans by surprise.

Wickland led Smith and Stevens on hands and knees toward a bathroom and then tried to seal the gap between the door and tile floor with towels. Opening the bathroom window brought in heavy diesel smoke instead of the fresh air he expected, so Wickland led the others on a low crawl back out into the hallway through the window of an adjoining bedroom inside the safe-haven area and onto a small patio, only to realize that he was alone.

About then, the two SEALs and the three other anxious GRS security officers waiting at the CIA annex adjusted their body armor and night-vision goggles as the tactical advantage of a quick counterattack slowly seeped away. Jack Silva heard one of the others say that it was time to stop waiting for permission and begin the counterattack. In the years since 2012, some have speculated that the GRS rescue operation might have been delayed that day to avoid revealing the CIA presence in Benghazi. Others have noted that if Silva, Woods, and the other GRS operators had gone to rescue the ambassador at the Diplomatic Compound, the CIA annex would be largely undefended. The call that put Silva, Woods, and the three others into motion came in at about 10:10 p.m. Benghazi time.

"If you guys don't get here, we're going to die."

Although highly trained and seasoned former SEALs, Woods and Silva didn't know who or what they faced. Despite the uncertainty, at least one of the five GRS operators was looking forward to action as the Mercedes and the BMW went out the CIA annex gate. Tanto spotted a small family of turtles living just outside the gate and smiled as if to tell them that he would be back.

Back at the Diplomatic Compound, Wickland fought off the temptation to panic. He tried twice to find Stevens and State Department communications officer Sean Smith in the smoke-filled bedrooms at the villa, even as the attackers sacked the cantina and tried once more to break down the barricades protecting the safe haven. Now desperate, Wickland climbed out of the villa and onto the roof using a ladder he found nearby. He alerted security officers in the Tactical Operations Center fifty yards away that he couldn't find the ambassador.

Tyrone Woods, Jack Silva, and the rest of the rescue team pondered the dangers while driving toward Wickland. They still didn't know whether the February 17th militia would be there and whose side the militia might take. And even if the militia supported the Americans, they might accidentally pepper the Americans with friendly fire.

Woods, Silva, and the other rescuers considered all this as they approached the Fourth Ring Road around Benghazi and slowly weaved through cars and pedestrians, eyes riveted on the Diplomatic Compound several hundred yards ahead.

Not knowing whether the February 17th militia might welcome or attack them, the Americans coming to rescue Ambassador Stevens picked the stealthiest route to the Diplomatic Compound. Now, in darkness ahead, on the road leading to the front gate, they spotted several men wearing black ski masks slouched against yet another technical. Silva wondered whether these were the militia friendlies who were supposed to meet them.

The BMW and Mercedes carrying the American rescuers ground to a halt as someone inside the compound begged on the radio for help yet again, reporting fires nearby. Henry, the interpreter drafted for this mission, confirmed that the men in the ski masks were "friendly" February 17th militiamen as gunfire from inside the compound increased. Despite worries about the loyalty and competency of these militia fighters, the team leader began planning the insertion into the compound. He could see that the road from the stopping point to the compound's gate exposed them to enemy fire from the upper stories of buildings and houses nearby.

D. B. Benton, a former SWAT team member and a U.S. Marine, offered a good approach to the problem: get two of the seven rescuers into a high sniper position in a five-story building.

Two of the Libyans went with Benton and Tanto. While the four remaining rescuers approached the eight-foot wall surrounding the Diplomatic Compound, several Americans already inside searched the villa for Ambassador Stevens and Sean Smith but found neither. Attackers inside the compound now took defensive positions outside the compound's wall, firing toward Silva, Woods, and three other would-be rescuers 400 yards in the distance.

Silva watched the chaotic scene from an intersection as two RPGs drove off some attackers just outside the Diplomatic Compound's gate. The commander of the February 17th militia now refused to storm the compound but volunteered to negotiate with the attackers for a deal.

The American rescuers four football fields away from the Diplomatic Compound faced increasingly limited options. Silva and Woods knew something must be done—quickly. They walked as quietly as possible down a narrow road leading toward the compound past construction sites where ambushers eager to kill three Americans might be waiting and through groups of local residents who came out of their houses to see what the commotion was all about. Hoping to see inside the compound, Silva and Woods climbed to the top of a tall pile of dirt at a construction site about a football field away from the compound's gate, only to discover that they weren't quite high enough to see inside.

On the way back down, Silva and Woods met three Libyan militiamen who decided to join the dangerous mission, invited or not. Just as they neared the steel-covered gate inside a concrete archway, the American rescue team began taking AK-47 fire from someone in the darkness, but it stopped as quickly as it began.

D. B. Benton and Tanto scouted their prospective overwatch position with two Libyan militiamen who volunteered to join them but discovered that the overwatch was farther away from the Diplomatic Compound than they thought. Looking quickly around, they saw another building nearby, close enough to the compound for overwatch. They climbed upward, hoping for a clear line of vision.

From the fourth floor, minutes later Benton and Paronto could see the militia barracks, the ambassador's villa, and several other buildings blazing brightly inside the compound. They wondered whether any of the Americans inside the compound remained alive but realized that the line of vision from here was too limited to serve as a sniper overwatch and moved to the back (south) side of the compound.

Forty minutes after the attack began, a U.S. surveillance drone approached Benghazi, and two Marine security platoons in Spain began preparing for deployment; Secretary of State Clinton then called the Libyan president to request local assistance since no American forces were close enough to meet the emergency.

The Americans at Benghazi were expected to take care of themselves since the closest help—Air Force fighters stationed at Aviono, Italy—needed three hours to get there. Mark Geist, back at the CIA annex, no doubt asked himself when the next attack would come while a mile away seven Americans, including Ambassador Stevens, trapped in various buildings certainly wondered if they would live to see September 12.

The seven rescuers, split between the front gate and the back gate, began rushing into the Diplomatic Compound. Silva and former Marine Sergeant John "Tig" Tiegen ran through the massive front gate with Woods some twenty-five yards in front of the other rescuers to minimize the chances of being attacked from behind as much as possible. Flames everywhere and smoke rose to the sky as gunfire echoed. Within a few seconds, Woods, Silva, and Tiegen met up with several DS agents standing in front of the villa door just after yet another search for the ambassador inside the smoke and fire–filled building.

Silva barely recognized Scott Wickland, the State Department operative he had met here several days before. Covered in black soot and bare-footed in good clothes now turned into rags, Wickland climbed down from the villa roof to meet them. The other DS agent in residence, David Ubben, didn't look much better. Two SEALs and two DS agents shook their heads in disbelief as furniture inside the once-plush ambassadorial villa burned just behind them.

Former SEALs Woods and Silva rushed forward while exchanging glances, saying everything that needed to be said about the chances of finding anyone alive inside. Climbing through a window into the once-safe haven, Silva immediately encountered diesel smoke and intense heat emanating from once-pristine marble floors. His already damaged contact lenses dried out instantly as the duo worked out a search routine on the spot without even exchanging a word. Spreading out across the room in different directions, Woods and Silva periodically darted back to the window to gulp in the freshest air available to avoid fainting.

Finding no one there, the SEALs began methodically searching the villa, feeling their way along the hallways so filled with smoke that visibility was two feet or less. Searching everywhere, even under the burning furniture, the SEALs found no one as boots burned their feet in a darkness illuminated only by faint flashlights mounted on their rifle barrels. Eventually, Woods and Silva became separated in much the same way that Scott Wickland, Sean Smith, and Ambassador Stevens had lost contact with each other hours before.

Several February 17th militiamen now darted into the villa from the front door as Silva looked on from a nearby window. Within minutes, as Jack peered inside, two DS agents wearing gas masks dragged a third man behind them. After helping lift the body through the window, Silva checked vital signs, tried to administer CPR, and confirmed that Sean Smith was dead. All three men standing around Smith wondered whether the ambassador was still alive.

A few minutes later, Tyrone Woods and John Tiegen pointed their rifles through the front entrance to the villa, crouched, and crept their way through the heat and smoke in yet another search for Ambassador Stevens. They separated briefly, Woods became lost, but Tiegen eventually found him. Outside, looking at an orchard that might well be filled with enemy snipers, Woods and Tiegen wondered out loud whether they would leave the Diplomatic Compound alive just as a friendly Blue Guard militiaman walked into the open. Both Americans lowered their rifles.

Woods now moved from building to building inside, without drawing gunfire, from the cantina to the Tactical Operations Center, eventually joining up with Silva and the rescue team leader back at the villa without finding Stevens. Woods and Silva knew that it was only a matter of time until the silence ended.

Even as they listened to reports of attackers regrouping nearby for a second assault on the American compound, they began discussing the very real possibility that Ambassador Stevens wouldn't be found because he had been abducted or somehow escaped. Wherever Stevens might be, it was time to gather what was left of the computer equipment and return to the CIA annex. Doing that might be all too dangerous since many of the February 17th militia members who supposedly were providing covering fire disappeared. Woods and Silva loaded Sean Smith's body into the Mercedes SUV, wondering out loud about their own chances of surviving.

Just after he handed a radio to somebody in the Land Cruiser, Silva felt the whooshing sound of an RPG. Grenades began falling in the Diplomatic Compound at about 11:10 p.m. while the two American vehicles raced out the front gate. Former U.S. Ranger Paronto and a fifty-something February 17th militia member provided supporting fire as Silva thought back on his SEAL training days and struggled against twenty-plus pounds of body armor. Just after the operators still in the Diplomatic Compound assembled on the roof, the team leader ordered an immediate evacuation. Silva, Woods, and the others piled into the Mercedes SUV for the convoy back to the CIA annex.

The Land Cruiser filled with DS agents initially drove west, only to be flagged and turned around by a militiaman assumed to be friendly. Within seconds, they faced opposing forces of radical Islamists at the Ansar al-Sharia militia base of operations directly east of the American Diplomatic Compound. Despite two flattened tires, DS agent Scott Wickland steered, dodged, and weaved over center medians and curbs and through oncoming cars, arriving at the CIA annex shortly after 11:00 p.m. local time. The Mercedes took a left, driving west without headlights illuminated, back toward the intersection from which the operation was launched about an hour earlier. Now an entirely new group of armed militia members stood staring at them near the BMW the Americans had abandoned there earlier. One of the locals called for them to stop, but Woods ignored the militiaman and drove on toward the CIA annex. The Americans arrived there without incident.

Just after 12:06 a.m. Libya time, former Navy SEAL Glen Doherty and several others left Tripoli to reinforce the American forces at Benghazi. The State Department advised the White House that according to the U.S. embassy in Tripoli, Ansar al-Sharia claimed responsibility for the attack, a report that has never been verified. Within half an hour, Woods and other operators on rooftops counted at least six cars dropping men off about 300 yards to the east near the home of a family openly hostile to the Americans. Soon, using night-vision goggles in the darkness, one of the Americans counted nine military-aged men within 100 yards of the CIA annex. Concerned about the possibility of teenagers playing a dangerous game or even friendly militiamen, the Americans prepared their weapons but held their fire.

Minutes later, somebody lobbed a fused bomb over the wall near an outdoor improvised gym. The very instant it exploded, at least nine Libyans outside the eastern wall of the annex began firing. The Americans quickly responded as the number of attackers grew to as many as thirty before gradually subsiding about ten minutes after it began.

About fifteen minutes after the firefight at the CIA annex ended, six Libyans found Ambassador Stevens in the back rooms of the Diplomatic Compound's villa and rushed him to the Benghazi medical center less than two miles away. Doctors declared Stevens dead of smoke inhalation by 2:00 a.m., just about the time security reinforcements from Tripoli had arrived at Benghazi International Airport.

New attackers began arriving at a rendezvous point 300 yards east of the annex about 2:30 a.m. Within fifteen minutes, fifteen cars dropped some twenty armed men who soon began moving toward the Americans, following the very same paths and duplicating tactics the Americans had seen about two hours earlier. This time, a car crept slowly toward the back gate of the annex on the northernmost portion of the east wall in full sight of an American sniper on an annex rooftop.

Just as quickly as a man leapt out of the car with something in his hand, looking toward the annex gate, one shot took him out, prompting attackers to open fire on the Americans from the trees and shrubs. The Americans repelled two ten-minute attacks in two hours without taking any casualties. After that, the Americans anxiously waited for reinforcements from Tripoli in the ominous silence.

Former SEAL Glen "Bub" Doherty, one of the Tripoli team members, had known Jack Silva and Tyrone Woods for many years. A bachelor of forty-two who grew up in an affluent Boston suburb, Doherty learned to fly and then became a ski instructor before a chance encounter with several SEALs changed his life eighteen years earlier. He became a sniper and a medic, participated in the mission responding to the 2000 attack on the USS *Cole* in Yemen, did two Iraq tours, and became a contractor operator four years after the 9/11 attacks.

A convoy of about ten Libyan police vehicles arrived at the CIA annex two hours before daylight, driving past the very house where the annex attackers had first assembled less than four hours earlier. The seven men worked out the details of the coming evacuation. Inside one of the buildings, at about 5:50 a.m., the planners wondered whether sunrise one hour later would bring a third attack on the annex. At least one of the operators urged an immediate exit from this place.

Even though the evacuation from the CIA annex would be conducted in stages, everyone was directed through radio calls to gather their belongings and assemble at Building C. As Doherty climbed a ladder there to talk with his fellow SEAL alum Tyrone Woods, an RPG hit the north annex wall, killing them both. Unseen gunmen opened up on the Americans and started a mortar attack.

From the rooftop next door, Jack Silva could see the damage to Building C but not his SEAL friend Tyrone Woods. Silva now realized that the attackers knew the exact location of the most critical buildings in the CIA annex and could lob in several mortar rounds before invading the complex anytime they wanted to. Instead, the attackers simply faded away for reasons that remain unknown.

Everyone in the CIA annex, including Jack, began preparing again for the exit to Tripoli. He quickly packed his belongings but missed a small box containing his wedding ring. Minutes later, he passed the bodies carried down from the Building C rooftop. Jack knew that Woods was probably dead but didn't even know that his friend Glen Doherty was in Benghazi. Some fifty white Toyota technicals arrived at about six that morning, bristling with heavy machine guns. The Americans didn't know whether they faced friend or foe until one of the former Rangers lowered his weapon, gave the militia commander a thumbs-up, and, after a brief hesitation, got the same sign back from his Libyan counterpart. The Ranger gestured a thumbs-down toward a nearby field. A few minutes later, a four-man Libyan fire team dragged two flex-cuffed hostiles out of the bush for questioning, never to be seen again.

Dawn arrived at 6:22 the next morning, as a combined Libyan–American convoy moved toward Benghazi airport carrying three dead heroes and dozens of other men whose lives were changed forever.

The first evacuation plane couldn't carry everyone, so five SEALs, three of them dead, waited on the tarmac as the militia who brought them from the Annex squabbled with the militia that controlled the airport. Two CIA agents argued about whether one of them should stay behind to find out who attacked the Diplomatic Compound while a militia member drove their abandoned BMW away with a smile on his face.

Other Libyans, some of whom worked with the Americans for years, came to say good-bye. One, in tears, assured Silva and the others that someone would be held accountable for the four American deaths. Within an hour, friendly Libyan militia brought Ambassador Stevens's body to the airport—intact, unmarked, and respectfully covered with a sheet. About two hours later, a Libyan C-130 flew the rest of the Americans into Tripoli. In the months that followed, four State Department officials took administrative leave and began new jobs. A bipartisan congressional committee reported that no evidence of intentional delay or obstruction of rescue efforts could be found despite claims to the contrary by some CIA annex security Team members. Mitchell Zuckoff related the story from the perspective of the annex security Team in *13 Hours*, from which much of the story in this chapter has largely but not exclusively been derived.

However controversial the death of Ambassador Stevens remains, one thing is clear: former SEAL Jack Silva and the other contract CIA operators at Benghazi saved at least twenty American lives.

CHAPTER EIGHTEEN

Lightning Ops

FROM A DISTANCE, THE MOUNTAINS LOOKED LIKE PYRAMIDS OF DIFFER-
ent sizes built helter-skelter next to each other along a dry, dusty, wide
road filled with donkeys shouldering huge packs. Some donkeys also
carried riders wearing turbans or bright blue neck-to-ankle robes swel-
tering under an unforgiving sun. Dr. Dilip Joseph, the medical director of
Morning Star Development medical clinics in Afghanistan, had seen this
all before in ten trips here over the past three years from the coolness of
Colorado Springs, Colorado, 7,300 miles to the west.

That Wednesday, December 5, 2012 (or the previous Sunday as
the *New York Times* initially reported), just after lunch, Dilip, Rafiq an
Afghan doctor, and Farzad, a Morning Star driver, guided some students
to a school near Pul-i-assim. Near there, four Taliban stopped them and
pulled all three out of Fazad's four-door pickup truck. The kidnappers
blindfolded, gagged, and bound them for a drive into a nearby desert
valley. Forced to climb upward into the mountains, they walked for some
nine hours to a thatched hut as Dilip gradually came to accept the very
real possibility that he might soon be killed.

Nineteen-year-old Wallakah was one of the Taliban who had kidnapped them, but during the days that followed, he talked frequently
with Dilip. And in a sense they became almost friends. Wallakah joined
the Taliban when the government imprisoned his father for no reason at
all—or so Wallakah said. Now, Wallakah wondered out loud whether Dr.
Joseph could take him to the United States to get away from the Taliban

and make a fresh start. After moving around for three days, the ransom party settled in at a compound in the Qarghari district of Laghma province, some seventy miles east of Kabul. They stayed in a one-story house at the base of a mountain where six blankets attached to the ceiling served as the front door. Even though cell phone ransom negotiations with Morning Star went nowhere, Rafiq and Farzad left unharmed as Dilip wondered how long he had to live.

American intelligence officers at Bagram Air Base wondered the same thing but concluded on the basis of some intelligence reports that Dilip was in imminent danger, now surrounded by nine Taliban fighters.

A SEAL Team Six crew began a rescue mission just before 8:00 p.m. on December 7, marching four hours through primitive mountain footpaths toward their object. Petty Officer Nicolas (Nic) Checque, a native of Monroeville, Pennsylvania, led the way.

Just after midnight, a dog barking in the distance woke Dilip up as sheep nearby began bleating. Gunfire brought the nine or so Taliban around him to their feet.

The SEALs outside knew that this was a high-risk mission that would depend on aggression, surprise, speed, and more than a little luck. About twenty-five yards shy of the compound, a Taliban fighter spotted them and ran inside with Checque on his tail. Senior Chief Edward Byers was the second SEAL in. He had been in Afghanistan for about two months when this mission began. Later, Byers remembered charging through blankets used as a makeshift door right into the hands of a Taliban warrior just behind Nic. While wrestling the Taliban for his life, Byers called out for Dilip. After settling that Taliban's hash, Byers found Dilip, covered him with his own body armor, and then pinned yet another Taliban holding a grenade to a wall long enough for another SEAL to take him out.

Minutes later, it was over. Surrounded by dead Taliban on the floor, the SEALs secured all explosives in the room as Dilip walked out a free man—but at a terrible cost. Nic Checque, shot in the head during the assault, died long before the helicopter arrived at Bagram Air Base after a forty-minute flight.

Initially, the American press reported that five Taliban captors had died while fighting the SEALs. However, in a later interview, Dilip said that Wallakah, the young Taliban who had befriended him, was not killed during the rescue operation. Instead, Dilip recalled seeing Wallakah, the very Taliban who shot Nic Checque, sitting on the ground head down, with his hands around his knees. Minutes later, according to this later account, Dilip reentered the house where he was held captive and saw Wallakah lying dead in his own blood. Unofficially, American military officials speaking only on background denied Dilip's second version of events, noting that Dilip was disoriented when rescued, never reentered the house, and could not have seen Wallakah in the darkness, presumably because he did not carry night-vision goggles. Despite this controversy, on Monday, February 29, 2016, Edward Byers received the Medal of Honor from President Obama. He was the first living sailor to receive the Medal of Honor since the Vietnam War. Two other Navy SEALs have received the Medal of Honor, both posthumously: Michael Monsoor for heroic action in 2006 and Michael Murphy for valor during Operation Red Wings in Afghanistan the previous year. During that same interview, Byers honored his friend. Nic died, Byers said, a hero's death, giving his life to rescue another American.

Asked whether he planned to write a memoir or look for a movie deal, Byers would only repeat the words that appear at the entrance of certain clandestine units within JSOC:

The deed is all, not the glory.

The upscale mall could have been one from anywhere in the United States, boasting earth-toned tile floors and affluent shoppers moving from store to store. The Westgate Mall was the best place to shop in Nairobi, Kenya, and that attracted five masked assailants, as well as several relatives of Kenyan President Uhuru Kenyatta, during the noon hour on Saturday, September 21, 2013. Thirty-two hours later, on Sunday evening, gunfire could still be heard inside; the shooting continued until September 24.

At least three terrorists and more than seventy men, women, and children died by the time it was over; a pool of blood next to a children's shoe shop said it all. Al Shabab threatened to attack again in retaliation for operations conducted against them by Kenyan forces operating in Somalia. Abdulkadir Mohamed Abdulkadir, known as "Ikrima," was among the most prominent Al Shabab leader. And the SEALs were coming after him.

Exactly fourteen days after the Westgate Mall attack began in Nairobi, at about 2:00 on the morning of October 5, a young mother of two, named Fadumo, in Barawe, Somalia, heard gunfire coming from a two-story house near her own home on the Indian Ocean. Since the house was occupied by Al Shabab fighters, she had heard this before, but the explosions a few minutes later brought new worries. Some twenty SEALs from Team Six arrived in a speedboat flanked by three support vessels two years and five months after killing Osama bin Laden.

Another Barawe resident now watched the SEALs carrying large packs north of a mosque and moving toward the targeted house just before a lone Al Shabab fighter came out the front door to have a cigarette. After pretending he didn't see them, he came back outside shooting an AK-47 as half the SEALs broke down the front door. Once inside, they began searching room by room for Ikrima, encountering many more women and children than they expected to see.

And so they left as Ikrima watched from a window. His bodyguard and two senior Al Shabab commanders died, according to later announcements of the Somali defense minister and the United Nations. A Pentagon spokesman told the press that more raids against Al Shabab were being planned even as other operations began.

SEAL Team Six operators and other Special Operations commandos and Yemeni soldiers helicoptered into the Hadhramaut province of eastern Yemen near the Saudi border in the early morning hours of Tuesday, November 25, 2014, on a rescue mission. Al-Qaeda in the Arabian Peninsula (AQAP), formed five years earlier, was holding eight hostages in a cave nearby. Abdu Rabbu Mansour Hadi, the president of Yemen, had requested the mission two weeks earlier. Some two dozen Americans and several American-trained Yemenis dashed into the mountain darkness, killed seven AQAP militants, and evacuated six hostages by helicopter, according to published news reports. The mission would have been even more successful but for the apparently coincidental removal of five other hostages, including an American, to another location two days before the first known American ground raid in Yemen.

Twenty months later, yet another SEAL Team Six team, jumping from high altitude, rescued an American and an Australian kidnapped from the American University in Kabul, Afghanistan. The two male professors walking toward a guesthouse on Thursday, August 7, 2016, were abducted, allegedly by Taliban. Seven presumed Taliban died in a gunfight during the rescue, although few details have been released.

Four months later, a SEAL Team Six team challenged AQAP again, this time attacking AQAP headquarters in Bayda province, Yemen. Some sources say that JSOC began planning the mission just before the transition from President Obama to President Trump. The surprise dawn attack on Sunday, January 29, 2017, was launched against targeted buildings occupied by known supporters of AQAP. American intelligence officials identified at least three instances in which AQAP operatives had tried to detonate bombs aboard commercial American jetliners. Three AQAP leaders—Abdul al Dhabab, Sultan al Dhubab, and Seif al Nims—died along with eleven other AQAP fighters but at a heavy price.

Eight women and seven children also died, as did Chief Petty Officer William "Ryan" Owens. He previously earned three Bronze Stars and was on his twelfth deployment overseas when he died.

SEAL payback for Owens's death came on Tuesday, May 23, 2017, in the central governorate of Yemen. The site extraction mission was initiated with Yemeni government approval to seize computers, cell phones, and hard drives from an AQAP headquarters compound; the SEALs had never inserted deeper into Yemen. Once on the ground, the special operators called in an AC-130 gunship; at least seven al-Qaeda terrorists were killed by combining SEALs small-arms fire with precision air strikes. Sadly, some twenty-five civilians caught in the cross fire also died.

President Trump paid tribute to Chief Petty Officer Owens for all Americans when he said that "Ryan died as he lived, a warrior and a hero, battling against terrorism and securing our nation."

Afterword

TODAY, AS THIS IS WRITTEN IN LATE 2017, THE NAVY SEALs ARE more important than ever to the defense of the United States. SEALs and other American special warfare combatants have paid a particularly high price in the global war on terror that began after the 9/11 attacks on the World Trade Center in New York and the Pentagon in Washington. More than half of American combat fatalities since 2015 have been service members assigned to U.S. special operations units. In 2017 alone, SEAL Chief Petty Officer Kyle Milliken died fighting Al Shabaab partisans in Somalia, thus becoming the first U.S. service member killed in that country since the 1993 Black Hawk incident. One thing is certain: the brave SEALs who have been so important to protecting the United States since 1962 will in all likelihood play an increasingly important role in the decades to come.

GLOSSARY OF TERMS AND ABBREVIATIONS

A-1 Skyraider: An anachronistic 1940s piston-powered propeller-driven airplane operated by the U.S. Marine Corps, U.S. Air Force, and U.S. Navy. The Skyraider, nicknamed "Spad," was retired from service in the early 1970s.

AC-130: A U.S. Air Force gunship variant of the C-130 fixed-wing Hercules transport. Known as the Spectre and sometimes called the Stinger, the AC-130 typically operates at low altitude (often about 7,000 feet) in close air support missions.

AH-IT Sea Cobra: Also known as the Huey Cobra or the Snake, the AH-1T served as the primary Army attack helicopter until replaced by the AH-64 Apache in September 1975. The twin-engine version is the primary attack helicopter of the U.S. Marine Corps.

Air Rescue and Recovery Service (ARRS): Established as the Air Rescue Service under the Air Transport Command, the organization was redesignated as ARRS in January 1966 and replaced in 1993 by the Military Airlift Command and other organizations.

AK-47: The Kalashnikov automatic rifle is a selective fire, gas-operated .308-mm assault rifle developed in the Soviet Union in 1947. The effective range of the Kalashnikov is 300 yards. The standard magazine holds thirty rounds.

AKS-74U machine gun: A short assault rifle derived in the late 1970s from the AKS-47 for use as a personal defense weapon for tank, gun, and helicopter crews. Known to U.S. forces as the Krinkov, a Russian manufacturer produced it until 1997. Afghanis named it the Krinkov during the Soviet invasion that began in December 1979.

Al-Qaeda: A Sunni multinational militia founded by Osama bin Laden and Abdullah Azzam in 1988 to oppose the Soviet invasion of Afghanistan. The term means "The Base," "The Foundation," or "The Fundament," an archaic English term meaning "foundation" or "base." Al-Qaeda is comprised largely of Islamic extremists and Salafist jihadists.

Ansar al-Sharia: A Libyan organization dedicated to the implementation of Sharia law and founded in 2011. The group, led by Muhammad al-Zahawi, targeted specific Americans and Libyans for death and participated in the Benghazi attack the next year. Ansar al-Sharia announced that it was dissolving in late May 2017.

Army Cougar: A Mine Resistant Ambush Protected (MRAP) vehicle with three doors, a diesel engine with three-ton capacity, and four-wheel drive. Typically, the Cougar is equipped with an automatic transmission, dual air conditioners, and capacity to carry a driver, driver assistant, and four additional passengers. This MRAP may travel on road and off road, equipped with run-flat tires.

Basic Underwater Demolition/SEAL training: A twenty-four-week training course consisting of a three week-orientation and three seven-week components for physical conditioning, combat diving, and land warfare. Enlisted and officer personnel go through identical training. The overall objectives are to build stamina, leadership, and teamwork through two-man swimming teams and other techniques.

Black Hawk: Sikorsky Aircraft Corporation submitted the basic design for the Black Hawk helicopter in a competition initiated by the U.S. Army in 1972. The Black Hawk, designated as YUH-60A, was selected as the winner over the Boeing Vertol YUH-61 in 1976. The aircraft was named for a leader of the American Sauk Indian tribe.

Chinook 47: A tandem-rotor heavy-lift helicopter designed and inaugurated by Boeing Vertol and one of the few aircraft of the 1960s still in production. The Chinook is powered by twin engines, is equipped with a rear loading ramp and ventral cargo hooks, and has a top speed of 196 miles per hour. The Chinook was named for the Native American Chinookan people of the Pacific Northwest. The Chinook remains one of the fastest, heaviest-lifting helicopters in the American aviation fleet.

Composition C-2: An American plastic explosive originating in the 1940s with manufacturing roots in materials developed by the British used in the Gammon bomb and classified as Composition C when adapted for U.S. use during World War II. It was replaced by Composition C-3 in 1944.

Danish Demining Group: A unit of the Danish Refugee Council whose primary mission is clearing unexploded ordnance and land mines as well as reducing armed violence.

EA-6B Prowler: A four-seat, twin-engine electronic warfare airplane that has been in service since 1971. Produced by Grumman (now Northrop Grumman), the Prowler descended from the A-6A Intruder, the electronic warfare aircraft used by the Marine Corps and the Navy. The Prowler crew includes a pilot and three electronic countermeasure officers who control antiradiation missiles such as the AGM-88 HARM. The Prowler was discontinued by the Navy in June 2015 but will continue in Marine service until 2019.

EB-66 Destroyer: A Douglas light bomber modified from the Navy A-3 Skywarrior to replace the Douglas A-26 Invader.

EOD (Explosives Ordnance Disposal): A function carried out by U.S. Navy technicians equipped to deal with improvised, chemical, biological, and nuclear ordnance by conducting demolitions, integrated into Combatant Commanders of the Special Operations Forces as well as Navy, Marine, and Army warfare units. EOD technicians use scuba, rafts, and fast-roping to conduct their missions.

F-4 Phantom II: An American supersonic jet fighter bomber produced by McDonnell Aircraft Corporation for the U.S. Navy. The Phantom earned the nickname "MiG Killer" during the Vietnam War.

F-14 Tomcat: A Grumman supersonic two-seated fighter created for the U.S. Naval Fighter Experimental (VPX) program based on data compiled in combat against MiG fighters in Vietnam. The Islamic Republic of Iran Air Force used them against Iraq during the Iran-Iraq War. The Tomcat was replaced in late 2006 by the Boeing F/A-18E/F Super Hornet.

February 17th Martyrs Brigade: A Libyan brigade of about twelve battalions that assisted U.S. forces and diplomats during the September 11, 2012, Benghazi attacks. The brigade was financed by the Libyan government and carried out self-directed missions in Kufra, Libya. The group was named in honor of Benghazians who attacked the Italian consulate after diplomat Robert Calderoli publicly defended the principle of free speech practiced in the Western world.

.50 mm: A machine gun (heavy) that is frequently installed on SEAL equipment.

FLIR (forward-looking infrared): A thermographic camera that senses infrared radiation vastly superior to standard night-vision devices.

Gap Assault Teams: Combined Army/Naval Combat Demolition Unit forces assigned to the Special Engineer Task Force for the D-Day Invasion, June 6, 1944.

Ghost Hawk: A medium-lift stealth version of the Black Hawk helicopter.

GPS (Global Positioning System): A space-based radio-navigation system that provides detailed data for military and civilian operations of the U.S. government.

Gravel: Vietnam War–era bomblets about the size of a lemon.

Hagensen Pack: A World War II–vintage C-2 explosive small enough to roll into an Army sock connected to a length of detonation cord. Hagensen Packs were used to clear beach obstacles on D-Day during the Normandy invasion.

Hanoi Hilton: The American nickname for the Hoa Lo prison in Hanoi originally used by the French for political prisoners in 1886 during the French colonial era. North Vietnam imprisoned American prisoners there during the Vietnam War. All that remains today is the guardhouse. Hoa Lo means "fiery furnace," a reference to the many stores selling stoves nearby.

Heckler & Koch MP-7: A German machine gun pistol used by the SEALs since 2001. The MP7 was designed to pierce body armor.

HH-3A: The Sikorsky SH-3 Sea King helicopter introduced in 1961 for antisubmarine warfare search-and-rescue and utility operations until 2006.

HH-3E helicopter (Jolly Green Giant or Jolly Green Sikorsky): A Vietnam-era helicopter designed by the Air Force to perform combat search-and-rescue operations for downed airmen. The CH-3 version carried armored plating and armament. The HH-3 version could land on water.

H&K 416: The Heckler & Koch (H&K) 416 became well known as the gun that U.S. Navy SEALs used to kill Osama bin Laden. The assault rifle/carbine was based on the AR-15 (M-16) class of weapons but uses a proprietary short-stoke gas piston system derived from an earlier Heckler & Koch G36 group of rifles.

Hellfire missile: An air-to-surface missile first developed for antiarmor purposes. Later variations were created for targeted killings of individuals, with air, sea, ground, and Predator drone launching capability. The AGM-114 was originally called the Heliborne Laser Fire-&-Forget missile but was eventually renamed the Hellfire. Weighing in at about 108 pounds and slightly over five feet in length, the Hellfire has been used from Vietnam to Afghanistan.

Humvee: The High Mobility Multipurpose Wheeled Vehicle, usually called the Humvee, was introduced in 1984 to replace Vietnam-era jeeps, was used in the Gulf War of 1991, and inspired a civilian version called the Hummer.

HVT (high-value target): A person or resource that SEALs and other special operators are often asked to capture alive if possible but neutralize if necessary. Examples in recent history include Osama bin Laden and former Iraqi President Saddam Hussein.

Intelligence Coordination and Exploitation Program (ICEX): An operation developed by Senior Vietnam CIA adviser Nelson Brickham Jr. after researching the counterinsurgency experiences of French officer David Galula from 1956 through 1958 during the Algerian War. ICEX was created in 1967 to gather information on the North Vietnamese–sponsored National Liberation Front. The South Vietnamese partner program was called Phung Hoang, honoring a mythical bird said to bring prosperity and luck. Later in 1967, ICEX was renamed the Phoenix Program.

ISIS: Jama'at al Tawhid wal-Jihad began as a group that in 1999 pledged allegiance to al-Qaeda, which participated in the Iraqi insurgency following the 2003 Western invasion. ISIS declared itself an Islamic state and a worldwide caliphate in June 2014, claiming religious, military, and political authority over all Muslims.

Islamic State of Iraq and the Levant (ISIL): Sometimes called the Islamic State of Iraq and Syria, or Daesh, a term derived from its Arabic acronym is an Arabic Salafi jihadist militant organization that follows a fundamentalist Wahhabi doctrine of Sunni Islam. ISIL drove the Iraqi government out of western Iraq and Mosul.

ISR (intelligence, surveillance, and reconnaissance): A process sometimes called ISTAR that links battlefield operations or functions together through systemic human and electronic battlefield observation. The techniques used include surveillance target acquisition and reconnaissance. Information gathered is passed on to intelligence analysts who refine the data for command situational awareness and the formulation of battle plans.

Joint Functional Component Command for Intelligence, Surveillance and Reconnaissance (JFCC ISR): A component of the Unified Combatant Commands colocated with the Defense Intelligence Agency. The JFCC ISR plans, executes, and assesses intelligence, surveillance, and reconnaissance operations to provide key decision makers with global situational awareness.

KH-12 Keyhole: An acronym for "Keyhole-class" (KH) reconnaissance satellites deployed for military missions. The KH-12 physically resembles the Hubble Space Telescope and is supported by Lacrosse-class radar-imaging satellites.

Khat: A green, flowering plant found from the Arabian Peninsula to the Horn of Africa that has been used as a stimulant for thousands of years. Khat is a controlled substance in Canada, Germany, the United Kingdom, and the United States that produces loss of appetite, euphoria, and dependence. Use of khat is legal in Kenya, Uganda, Ethiopia, Somalia, Yemen, and Israel.

Landing Craft, Personnel (Large) (LCPL): A landing craft developed in 1940 and used throughout World War II to deploy thirty-six-man infantry platoons. The LCPL was crewed by three men, traveled at eight knots (nine miles) per hour, and was unloaded at the beach over the sides or bow. Armament typically included Browning .30-caliber machine guns.

Landing Ship, Tank (LST): World War II–vintage ships that supported amphibious operations by landing troops, tanks, Jeeps, and cargo directly onshore using a large bow door and ramp system. The LST was equipped with a flat keel, twin propellers, and rudders equipped to avoid grounding.

M48 tank: Called the Patton, this tank was developed during World War II and in service until entirely replaced by the M60. The M48 saw action in Vietnam and was used in NATO countries.

MH-53 Pave Low: A long-range combat search-and-rescue helicopter derived from the Sikorsky CH-53 Sea Stallion for use in special operations missions. The U.S. Air Force version was retired in April 2008. Pave Low was used for long-range low-level covert penetration into denied areas for infiltration, exfiltration (extraction), and resupply of special operations forces.

Military Assistance Command, Vietnam–Studies and Observations Group (MACV-SOG): A multiservice special operations unit that conducted unconventional warfare operations in Vietnam, Laos, and Cambodia. Missions included capturing enemy prisoners, conducting rescue operations to retrieve prisoners of war and downed pilots, clandestine agent team activities, and psychological operations. MACV-

SOG participated in the Gulf of Tonkin operation, the Tet Offensive, and other initiatives before being replaced by the Strategic Technical Directive Assistance Team in May 1972.

MK 11: A sniper rifle derived from the SR-25 by the U.S. Special Operations Command to include a twenty-inch barrel capable of firing M118 NATO rounds. The MK11 also features a quick detachable sound suppressor mount, flip-up front sights, and pistol grips.

Mujahideen (Muj): A plural version of Mujahid, an Arabic term for one engaged in striving or struggling for a praiseworthy aim (Jihad). The term was originally associated with Islamist military units that challenged Soviet military during the Soviet-Afghan War but is now used to describe Afghans whom SEALs and other American forces faced in Mideast military operations after 9/11.

Naval Combat Demolition Unit (NCDTU): An organization created in the late winter of 1943 to eliminate obstacles on enemy-held beaches and clear paths for incoming landing craft. These units were to operate from boats rather than as swimmers. The trainees called themselves "Demolitioneers." Army Scout and Raider personnel who earlier received British Commando training conducted the initial NCDTU training before the program was discontinued in the spring of 1944.

Naval Special Warfare Command (NAVSPECWARCOM): The naval component of the U.S. Special Operations Command, also known as NSWC. It is the unified command responsible for overseeing and conducting the nation's special operations and missions, including unconventional warfare, direct action, counterterrorism, special reconnaissance, and rescue. NSWC is comprised of some eight Navy SEAL teams, three special boat teams, and various supporting commands, totaling about 9,000 who operate independently, in amphibious ready groups, or integrated with other U.S. special operations forces. Navy ships and submarines provide rapid deployment worldwide.

NODs (night optic devices): Optoelectronic devices producing images despite total darkness used by law enforcement and military organizations using telescopic lenses and mirrors and illuminators.

Nongovernmental organization: A not-for-profit organization independent from national and international government, funded by donations and often run by volunteers.

North Vietnamese Army: A term often used by Americans for the People's Army of Vietnam, which was established and headquartered in Hanoi and captured Saigon in late April 1975.

NVGs (night-vision goggles): Devices used to produce high levels of light when observing objects in total darkness, using near-infrared thermal imaging. Modern NVGs are used by infantry, special operators, drivers, and aviators.

OBL: Osama bin Laden.

1152 HMMWV: A *High Mobility Multipurpose Wheeled Vehicle* troop carrier enhanced with Integrated Armor Protection to serve as a cargo or troop carrier, carrying as many as eight passengers. The 1152 payload varies from 3,300 to 5,100 pounds, depending on equipment and armament installed.

O-2 Skymaster: A military version of the Cessna 337 Super Skymaster, nicknamed "Oscar Deuce," used for forward air control and psychological operations by the U.S. military between 1967 and 2010.

Ops: Operations.

Orion P-3: A four-engine antisubmarine, reconnaissance, and maritime surveillance plane derived from the Lockheed L-188 Electra commercial airliner in the 1960s that has been used for more than fifty years of continuous service.

OV-10 Bronco: A turboprop light attack and observation airplane developed by North American Rockwell for counterinsurgency and forward air control service capable of carrying troops or three tons of munitions for as long as three hours.

PBR (Patrol Boat, River): A small rigid-hulled patrol boat used in the Mekong Delta, Rung Sat Special Zone, I Corps region, in the northernmost region of South Vietnam and on the Saigon River by the U.S. Army 458th Transportation Company (Seatigers) to insert and extract Navy SEAL teams.

Phoenix Program: Officially created in 1967 as the Intelligence Coordination and Exploitation Program (ICEX), Phoenix was designed, coordinated, and implemented by the U.S. Central Intelligence Agency, U.S. Special Operations Forces, U.S. Army intelligence operations units, and Republic of Vietnam (South Vietnam) special operations units to capture and neutralize Vietcong operatives, informants, and supporters. Some sources estimate that some 82,000 such targets were neutralized, of whom some 26,000 to 41,000 were killed in this controversial program.

Provincial Reconnaissance Units: South Vietnamese military who maintained regional interrogation centers and killed or captured Vietcong and their sympathizers.

Rocket-propelled grenade (RPG): An antitank weapon system that fires rockets equipped with explosive warheads initially designed by Russia. The RPG is shoulder fired for use against tanks and armored personnel carriers, using high-explosive antitank warheads capable of causing secondary damage to tracks, roofs, and turrets, even when there is no penetration of the target.

Rung Sat Special Zone: A region of Vietnam now known as the Can Gio Mangrove Forest. The name is derived from the term "salty forest," referencing saltwater marshes nearby.

S-75 Dvina: A high-altitude Soviet air defense system first deployed in 1957. The system incorporated a surface-to-air missile with command guidance.

Sapper: Also known as a pioneer or combat engineer who conducts breaching, demolition, bridge building, minefield clearing, airfield construction, and repair in both offensive and defensive operations.

Seabees: U.S. Naval Construction Battalions: Sailors trained to conduct combat-related construction operations and engage in combat if necessary in multiple combat theaters.

SEAL Delivery Vehicle (SDV): A manned submersible that is flooded and used to deliver Navy SEALs and SEAL equipment for special operations in areas held by hostile forces or where military activity would draw attention and objection. The SEAL swimmers ride exposed to the water, breathing either through scuba gear or using compressed air carried on the SDV. A larger dry submersible, called the Advanced SEAL Delivery System, includes an air-conditioning system.

Search and Rescue: Missions sometimes designated combat search and rescue carried out by task forces consisting of helicopters and ground-attack aircraft supported by refueling tankers and airborne command forces and often using U.S. Air Force HC-130s.

Sensitive-site exploitation: A series of activities inside a captured sensitive site to exploit electronic data, files, and personnel records.

South Vietnamese Army Company: An alternative name for the Army of the Republic of Vietnam, the ground troops of the Republic of Vietnam military forces of South Vietnam from 1955 to April 1975.

Special Operations Command: The Unified Combatant Command created by the U.S. Congress to oversee Special Operation Component Commands of the Army, Marine Corps, Air Force, and Navy, headquartered at MacDill Air Force Base, Tampa, Florida. It conducts several covert and clandestine missions, such as direct action, special reconnaissance, counterterrorism, foreign internal defense, unconventional warfare, psychological warfare, civil affairs, and counternarcotics operations.

SR-71 Blackbird: A strategic reconnaissance aircraft derived from the Lockheed A-12. The Blackbird operates at high altitudes and is capable of outrunning air-to-surface missiles.

Stealth Hawk: Sikorsky UH-60 Black Hawk helicopters that incorporate stealth technology to minimize rotor blade noise and radar visibility.

Strip charge: A high-efficiency explosive used to blow open wooden doors and glass windows.

Surface-to-air missile (SAM): An antiaircraft weapon partially developed during World War II but not implemented. The first operational SAM was the Nike Ajax, followed by the Russian S-75 Dvina, the latter being the most widely distributed and used. Short-range shoulder-launched SAMs include the Stinger and the Strela-3.

Technical: Open-backed civilian open-bed trucks and four-wheel-drive vehicles equipped with machine guns, antiaircraft guns, rotary cannons, mortars, or rocket launchers serving as improvised light military gun vehicles. Describing such a vehicle as a "technical" began in Somalia when money allocated for technical assistance grants from nongovernmental organizations was used instead for this purpose.

Bibliography

Anderson, William C. *Bat-21*. Englewood Cliffs, NJ: Prentice Hall, 1989.

Andrade, Dale. *Ashes to Ashes: The Phoenix Program*. Lexington, MA: Lexington Books, 1990.

Bahmanyar, Mir, with Chris Osman. *SEALs: The US Navy's Elite Fighting Force*. Oxford: Osprey Publishing, 2008.

Blehm, Eric. *Fearless: The Undaunted Courage and Ultimate Sacrifice of Navy SEAL Team SIX Operator Brown*. New York: WaterBrook, 2013.

Boehm, Roy, and Charles W. Sasser. *First Seal*. New York: Pocket Books, 1987.

Bowden, Mark. *Black Hawk Down: A Story of Modern War*. New York: Atlantic Monthly Press, 1999.

Bragg, Rick. *I Am a Soldier Too: The Jessica Lynch Story*. New York: Knopf, 2003.

Buchanan, Jessica, Erik Landemalm, and Anthony Flacco. *Impossible Odds: The Kidnapping of Jessica Buchanan and Her Dramatic Rescue by SEAL Team Six*. New York: Atria Books, 2014.

Chun, Clayton. *Gothic Serpent: Black Hawk Down: Megadishu 1993*. London: Osprey Publishing, 2012.

Couch, Dick. *Down Range: Navy SEALs in the War on Terrorism*. New York: Three Rivers Press, 2005.

———. *The Sheriff of Ramadi: Navy Seals and the Winning of al-Anbar*. Annapolis, MD: Naval Institute Press, 2010.

Couch, Dick, and William Doyle. *Navy SEALS: Their Untold Story*. New York: William Morrow, 2014.

Darak, Ed. *Victory Pont: Operations Red Wings and Whalers: The Marine Corps' Battle for Freedom in Afghanistan*. New York: Berkley Publishing Group, 2009.

Dockery, Kevin. *The Navy SEALS: A History of the Early Years*. New York: Berkley Publishing Group, 2001.

———. *Navy Seals II: The Viet Nam Years*. New York: Berkley Publishing Group, 2002.

———. *Navy Seals: The Complete History*. New York: Berkley Publishing Group, 2004.

———. *Operation Thunderhead: The True Story of Vietnam's Final POW Rescue Mission—and the Last Navy SEAL Killed in Country*. New York: Berkley Publishing Group, 2008.

Emerson, Clint. *100 Deadly Skills: The SEAL Operative's Guide to Eluding Pursuers, Evading Capture and Surviving Any Dangerous Situation*. New York: Touchstone, 2015.

Geraghty, Tony. *Black Ops*. New York: Pegasus Books, 2010.

Green, Daniel R. *In the Warlords' Shadow: Special Operations Forces, the Afghans, and Their Fight against the Taliban*. New York: Threshold Editions, 2017.

Hersh, Seymour. *The Killing of Osama Bin Laden*. London: Verso, 2016.

Kerrey, Bob. *When I Was a Young Man*. New York: Harcourt, 2002.

Kyle, Chris. *American Sniper: The Autobiography of the Most Lethal Sniper in U.S. Military History*. New York: HarperCollins, 2012.

Lacz, Kevin, with Ethan E. Rocke and Linsey Lacz. *The Last Punisher: A SEAL Team THREE Sniper's True Account of the Battle of Ramadi*. New York: Threshold Editions, 2016.

Luttrell, Marcus, with Patrick Robinson. *Lone Survivor: The Eyewitness Account of Operation Redwing and the Lost Heroes of SEAL Team TEN*. New York: Little, Brown, 2013.

Marcinko, Richard, with John Weisman. *Rogue Warrior: The Explosive Autobiography of the Controversial Death-Defying Founder of the Navy's Top-Secret Counterterrorist Unit—Seal Team Six*. New York: Pocket Books, 1992.

Mooney, Michael J. *The Life and Legend of Chris Kyle: American Sniper, Navy SEAL*. New York: Back Bay Books, 2013.

Norris, Tom, and Mike Thornton with Dick Couch. *By Honor Bound: Two Navy SEALs, the Medal of Honor and a Story of Extraordinary Courage*. New York: St. Martin's Press, 2016.

O'Neill, Robert. *The Operator: Firing the Shots That Killed Osama Bin Laden and My Years as a SEAL Team Warrior*. New York: Scribner, 2017.

Owen, Mark, and Kevin Maurer. *No Easy Day: The Firsthand Account of the Mission That Killed Osama Bin Laden*. New York: New American Library, 2014.

Pfarrer, Chuck. *Warrior Soul: The Memoir of a Navy SEAL*. New York: Random House, 2004.

———. *Seal Target Geronimo: The Inside Story of the Mission to Kill Osama Bin Laden*. New York: St. Martin's Press, 2011.

Phillips, Richard, with Stephan Talty. *A Captain's Duty: Somali Pirates, Navy SEALS and Dangerous Days at Sea*. New York: Hyperion, 2010.

Stone, Steve. *Afghan Warrior: U.S. Navy Seal's Stores of Valor in Afghanistan*. Los Gatos, CA: Digital Dreams Publishing, 2016.

Valentine, Douglas. *The Phoenix Program*. New York: William Morrow, 2000.

Veith, George J. *Code-Name Bright Light: The Untold Story of U.S. POW Rescue Efforts during the Vietnam War*. New York: Dell Publishing, 1998.

Wasdin, Howard E., and Stephen Templin. *SEAL Team Six: Memoirs of an Elite Navy SEAL Sniper*. New York: St. Martin's Press, 2011.

Webb, Brandon, with John David Mann. *The Red Circle: My Life in the Navy SEAL Sniper Corps and How I Trained America's Deadliest Marksmen*. New York: St. Martin's Paperbacks, 2014.

———. *Among Heroes: A U.S. Navy SEAL's True Story of Friendship, Heroism, and the Ultimate Sacrifice*. New York: NAL CALIBER, 2015.

Whitcomb, Darrel D. *The Rescue of Bat 21*. Annapolis, MD: Naval Institute Press, 2014.

Zimmerman, Dwight. "Lieutenant-Colonel Iceal Hambleton." *The Times* (London), October 1, 2004.

Zimmerman, Dwight Jon, and John Gresham. *Beyond Hell and Back: How America's Special Operations Forces Became the World's Greatest Fighting Unit*. New York: St. Martin's Griffin, 2008.

Zuckoff, Mitchell. *13 Hours: The Inside Account of What Really Happened in Benghazi*. New York: Hatchette Book Group, 2014.